Hospitality Mana

Related Macmillan titles

The New Catering Repertoire H. L. Cracknell and G. Nobis
   Volume 1 Aide-Mémoire du Chef
   Volume 2 Aide-Mémoire du Restaurateur et Sommelier
Practical Professional Catering H. L. Cracknell, G. Nobis and
                                R. Kaufmann
Practical Professional Cookery H. L. Cracknell and R. Kaufmann
Practical Professional Gastronomy H. L. Cracknell and G. Nobis
Managing Food Hygiene Nicholas Johns
Healthy Eating: a guide for chefs and caterers Rob Silverstone

In the Mastercraft series, published with the Hotel and Catering Training Company:

Customercraft: Keeping the Customer Satisfied Roy Apps
Foodcraft 1: The Dry Processes
Foodcraft 2: The Wet Processes
*Mastercraft 1: Working in the Hotel and
                Catering Industry* Sally Messenger
*Mastercraft 2: Health, Hygiene and Safety
                in the Hotel and Catering Industry* Marion Kenber and
                                        William McCurrach

Professional Masters – all the professional student needs – in a single text:

Basic English Law W. T. Major
Communication Nicki Stanton
Company Accounting Roger Oldcorn
Cost and Management Accounting Roger Hussey
Employee Relations Chris Brewster
Management Roger Oldcorn
Marketing Robert I. Maxwell
Personnel Management Margaret Attwood
Study Skills Kate Williams
Supervision Mike Savedra and John Hawthorn

Please write to The Sales Department, Macmillan Education, Houndmills, Basingstoke, Hants, for details of other Mastercraft titles, other Macmillan textbooks and the current Further and Continuing Education catalogue.

Hospitality Management
Case Study Assignments

Sally Messenger

Lecturer in Hotel Management,
Department of Management Studies for Tourism and Hotel Industries,
University of Surrey

and

Humphrey Shaw

Senior Lecturer in Accounting and Finance,
The Business School,
Polytechnic of North London

MACMILLAN

First published 1991

Published by
MACMILLAN EDUCATION LTD
Houndmills, Basingstoke, Hampshire RG21 2XS
and London
Companies and representatives
throughout the world

Edited and typeset by Povey/Edmondson
Okehampton and Rochdale, England

Printed in Hong Kong

British Library Cataloguing in Publication Data
Messenger, Sally
Hospitality management: case study assignments
1. Restaurants. Management 2. Hotels. Management
I. Title II. Shaw, Humphrey
647.95068
ISBN 0–333–54683–0

Contents

Introduction   vii

PART I   FOOD AND BEVERAGE MANAGEMENT

1   On-Line   2
2   The Do Drop Inn   8
3   Bridley City General Hospital   12
4   Newland Town Hall   14
5   The String of Pearls   20

PART II   FRONT OFFICE AND ACCOMMODATION MANAGEMENT

6   Hamilton College of Further Education   30
7   Countrywide Manors   34
8   Clevden Residential Management Centre   38
9   The Lord Dubarry   42
10 The Dunadry   48

PART III HUMAN RESOURCES MANAGEMENT

11 The Grand Hotel   52
12 The Carlton Hotel   60
13 Inn on the Lake   70
14 The Valley View Hotel   74
15 Kirby Lodge   80

PART IV MARKETING

16 Travel Pal   88
17 Blaen Wern   92
18 Crown Hotels   98
19 The Cedar Tree Hotel   102
20 Truffles   106

PART V FINANCIAL MANAGEMENT

21   The Riverside Inn   112
22   Falmer School   118
23   Griffin Hotel and Leisure Group   122
24   Beinn Bhalgairean and Kinglass Hotels   130
25   The Catering Hire Company   136

PART VI OPERATIONS MANAGEMENT

26   City of Lights Hotel   140
27   The Salad Bowl   146
28   Fit-For-Living Leisure Centre   150
29   The Seven Bridges   154
30   The Rice House   158

Acknowledgements

The authors would like to acknowledge the help of John Coshall and Robert Slack, both Senior Lecturers in Quantitative Methods at the Business School, Polytechnic of North London, in the composition of this book. Amanda Page and Sue Badger helped with the typing and Sue Kitching aided the authors with the proof-reading.

Note: The names and addresses of all the people and businesses in this book are invented, and any resemblance to any actual person or business is entirely coincidental.

This book is dedicated to our parents

Introduction

How to Approach the Case Studies

The case studies have been designed to assist you in applying management theories and concepts to real-life situations. They aim to develop your competence in analytical and problem-solving skills. Each case integrates different management issues and draws on your knowledge of:

> Food and Beverage Management
> Front Office and Accommodation Management
> Human Resource Management
> Marketing Management
> Financial Management
> Operations Management

Method of Approach

A logical and sequential approach should be adopted when dealing with case studies. The flow chart overleaf illustrates the steps that should be taken and the process that should be followed.

10 Key points

(1)

Read the case questions to gain an immediate insight into the management areas being investigated.

(2)

Read the case carefully and establish the central problem. Clearly distinguish between symptoms and causes.

(3)

Determine any secondary problems.

(4)

Decide which factors in the case will have a bearing on the answer(s).

(5)

Establish the theoretical areas of knowledge that underpin the case.

(6)

Determine the range of courses of action that could be taken and test the anticipated effects of each course.

(7)

Select one course of action and give reasons for your choice.

(8)

Decide how the course of action could be implemented.

(9)

Indicate the factors that should be taken into consideration when presenting the case answer(s).

(10)

Outline how the solution could be evaluated.

Part I
Food and Beverage Management

1 On-Line

Introduction

Contract catering is a significant sector of the UK hospitality industry. As more companies enter the marketplace the greater the need to provide a first class product and service to their client companies.

Aims

To develop analytical skills in assessing the strengths, weaknesses, opportunities and threats of an individual operation.

Competences Required for this Case

(a) Theoretical knowledge of the contract catering concept;
(b) Ability to identify underlying causes of problems;
(c) Ability to highlight areas for potential success; and
(d) Creativity in developing solutions and practical business advice.

On-Line is a market leader in writing computer software for the hotel and catering industry. It has overseas offices in Brussels, New York and Paris and employs a total of 3000 staff. Its UK office is based in Cambridge, where 360 people are employed.

The company chairman, Mr Bryan Huckle, has always believed in looking after his staff well and since becoming chairman he has introduced a number of initiatives designed to improve the working conditions of his employees. The first initiative he introduced was a company health and welfare facility which offers employees the opportunity to participate in a private health scheme, the cost being subsidised by the company. He has also given the go-ahead for the development of company leisure centres offering gyms, saunas, swimming pools and squash courts. All staff and their families may use these facilities without charge. Finally Mr Huckle has introduced a subsidised catering service for all employees, with outside caterers being responsible for providing the service.

At the Cambridge office the catering operation is managed by Caterplus, a national organisation specialising in providing catering services for companies in the south of England. Caterplus have held the On-Line contract for the past three years. The chef/manager, Marcos Rossini, is in charge of the administration and cooking, assisted by food service assistants Flori, Paul, Matilda and Elsie, plus Ralph the kitchen porter, and Daisy, the cashier. The restaurant seats eighty people and operates on a self-service system. It is heavily subsidised by On-Line and the prices are as follows:

Starters	15p
Main course	35p
Sweets	15p
Coffee/tea	10p

When the restaurant opened three years ago the staff queued to get a seat but this is no longer the situation. The client contact at On-Line, Cynthia Diamond has received a number of comments from staff saying they are no longer happy with the catering service. Cynthia has been in touch with Joanna Noble, the operations director of Caterplus, to inform her that the problems must be dealt with before the contract is re-negotiated at the end of the following month. Cynthia received the following fax from Joanna.

FAX COVER SHEET

To: Cynthia Diamond, Client Contact	Fax 013-445 9987

Company name   On-Line

From:	Joanna Noble, Operations Director	Fax 014-223 0734
	Caterplus	

Date 9.6.91	Time 15.05

Number of pages including this sheet   1

Re this morning's telephone conversation I have now spoken to Marcos Rossini and I suggest we all meet tomorrow afternoon at your offices at 14.30. Please let me know if this time is convenient.

Joanne Noble

In the event of poor
transmission phone: 014-337 1653

After reading the fax Cynthia gave some thought as to what items should be on the agenda for the afternoon meeting. She drew up the following list of points which she wished to raise with Joanna:

1. Menu has become boring. The staff always know what will be on the menu each day.
2. Not enough choice of main courses. Only one hot and cold dish each day.
3. High calorific content of most meals.
4. Slow service with 20 minutes being the average queueing time.
5. Poor standard of hygiene with tables not being cleared regularly, and complaints about dirty cutlery and crockery.

The next day Joanna arrived at 2 pm at On-Line and made her way to the restaurant, where she met Marcos, whom she had asked to meet for half an hour to discuss the matter before their joint meeting with Cynthia. Joanna asked Marcos if he had any idea of what was making the client company unhappy with the standard of service. He replied that there had been some problems. Firstly, many of the suppliers had raised prices and it was now hard to provide the same quality of meals on such a limited budget. Also the staff were not happy with their pay, as recent rises in the industry meant that they were now underpaid for the work they did. Joanna thanked him for his comments and together they made their way to see Cynthia.

Cynthia	Perhaps I had better start the meeting by running through a list of comments that have been made to me frequently over the past couple of months. Here is a copy of the points for your own reference.

(*Cynthia handed Joanna the list which she had compiled the previous afternoon*)

Joanna	Thank you. Clearly the problem seems to be divided into two areas. As always, menu and service. I have talked about our current problems with Marcos and I know that he would like to outline the most urgent problems.
Cynthia	Please, Marcos, do tell me.
Marcos	Well, at the moment I have a problem with our suppliers. You see they all increased their prices last month. In some cases the increases were in the order of 10 per cent and that makes it nearly impossible to keep

	within my budget. Also, my staff complain that they are underpaid and some of the customers ask for double portions.
Cynthia	Well, this certainly puts a new angle on the problem. I didn't realise that all this was going on.
Joanna	May I suggest a way forward. In order to avoid discussing the issues at length, Cynthia, I would like to go back to head office and draw up a short-term and long-term strategy for the overall improvement of the catering service here. If its OK with you I will send you a draft copy by the end of the week and then we can have another meeting to finalise our plan.
Cynthia	Yes, that sounds like an excellent idea. Let my secretary know when you want the meeting. I look forward to discussing the plan with you.

On returning to her office Joanna telephoned you, as the special projects officer to ask your advice on what action should be taken at On-Line. You have agreed to produce a report outlining a strategy for improvement of the catering service at On-Line.

Points to be Considered when Dealing with this Case

Contract caters are often invited to manage the catering operations of organisations which prefer not to recruit and employ staff directly. In producing your report you should consider the following:

(a) The role of contract caterers:

- How do they function?
- What are the financial implications?
- How are they usually selected?
- What are their strengths?

(b) In drawing up the report, consider:

- Who will be reading the document?
- What will they be most interested in?
- How important is the document in relation to the renewal of the contract?

(c) In developing the short- and long-term strategies, identify those factors that:

- Can be resolved in the immediate future, and how.
- Cannot be resolved for a period of time – give your reasons and suggest the resources/support needed.

2 The Do Drop Inn

Management Theme: Determining the Viability of a Business Venture

Introduction

The hospitality industry is composed of a large number of small owner-managed businesses. Whilst not all of these individuals enter the industry with no previous experience of running a business, many do. As a result they need careful guidance on how to determine the feasibility of an idea and how to produce an associated plan for it.

Aims

To develop skills in highlighting the key points in carrying out a market feasibility study, drawing up a business plan and presenting these in a way that is easy to understand.

Competences Required for this Case

> (a) Theoretical knowledge of the purpose and content of a market feasibility study and a business plan; and
> (b) Ability to present interesting and comprehensive material in a clear, concise and logical format.

The Do Drop Inn is situated in the heart of the Gloucestershire countryside. Major Henry Drummond and his wife, Penelope, bought the public house three years ago when Major Drummond retired from the Army. When they took the pub over the main trade was coming from local village people, but over the past two years the opening of a motorway nearby has brought new passing trade to the Inn.

Henry and Penelope are very pleased with the profit they have been making. Since taking over the Do Drop Inn they have seen profits increase by 20 per cent per year. The future, however, does not look quite so optimistic due to proposed new legislation affecting drinking and driving. The Government is determined to reduce the level of alcohol-induced accidents and is considering introducing new and stronger penalties for drivers found to be over the legal limit. Henry and Penelope have already noticed an increase in demand from customers for fruit juices, lemonades, tea and coffee, with a reduction in the number of pints of beer and measures of spirits being consumed.

The couple have given the matter serious thought and decided they ought to consider moving into the catering market. Penelope is a Cordon Bleu cook; she feels she could manage this side of the operation with perhaps an extra part-time member of staff. However, they do not want to rush into the project without being reasonably certain that it would be a success. The new venture would require a large amount of capital investment.

The Drummonds have mentioned their ideas to one of their customers, Phil Tipple. Phil is now retired but he used to be operations director for the brewery chain, Top Brew. His advice is to undertake a market feasibility study before proceeding with the project.

You work for the trade magazine *Food at the Bar*, and each week you produce a page of readers letters/enquiries. This week you have received the following letter from Penelope Drummond and a memo from your senior editor.

MEMORANDUM

From: Senior editor

To: Junior editor

We are getting a lot of the following letters from owners of country pubs. So far we have not responded but I would like you to write an article outlining how a market feasibility study and business plan can assist small businesses decide whether or not to proceed with a new venture.

The Do Drop Inn
Beaumont Village
Gloucestershire
GL2 6HJ

Dear Sir

I am writing to you for your advice on how I can undertake a market feasibility study. My husband and I own and manage a small country pub in the heart of Gloucestershire and we think we want to start offering food. We have not got the finance to pay for a study to be done and wondered if you could advise us on how we should go about this.

Yours faithfully,

Penelope Drummond

Penelope Drummond

Points to be Considered when Dealing with this Case

Small businesses often start by offering a new product or service without much market research, due to the costs of employing an external consultant. There is, therefore, a distinct need from this sector for basic advice which can help them gather necessary market research data, later to be translated into a business plan. In answering the case questions you should consider:

(a) The aims of a market feasibility study;

(b) The major areas to be covered by the study;

(c) External sources of information and assistance which are available; and

(d) The objectives of a business plan.

3 Bridley City General Hospital

Management Theme: Setting and Maintaining Food Hygiene and Safety Standards

Introduction

Health, safety and food hygiene legislation is increasing and becoming more stringent. Hospitality managers need to be aware of the importance of training and retraining their staff to meet the requirements and produce a safe product for their customers.

Aims

To develop skills in producing a training programme which will benefit staff, the organisation and customers.

Competences Required for this Case

(a) Theoretical knowledge of health, safety and hygiene legislation and guidelines; and

(b) Techniques of developing an effective training programme.

Claire Thomas the catering manager at Bridley City General Hospital looked at the article in the *Daily National* and sighed. The recent outbreak of food poisoning had led to more newspaper articles on the importance of hygiene in food preparation. The paper blamed catering staff working in local restaurants. Although there had been no cases of food poisoning at Bridley City General Hospital, Claire felt that the staff should be made aware of the health and safety aspects of food preparation.

The hospital was old, having been built in 1889, and the kitchens had not been modernised since the early 1970s. To make matters worse the hospital was operating at full capacity, putting a lot of pressure on the kitchen staff. Labour turnover amongst the younger catering staff was high. For a long time Claire had been worried that new staff needed to be trained in the importance of hygiene and safety in the kitchen.

You work at the hospital as assistant catering manager. Claire has asked you to develop a one-day training programme for all kitchen staff on the theme of 'How to work safely and hygienically in the kitchen'.

Points to be Considered when Dealing with this Case

Training programmes are one popular way of bringing staff up-to-date with health, safety and hygiene legislation. In developing the training programme you should consider:

(a) The current laws regarding the topic and the significant parts of the current legislation which will apply to staff;
(b) How the information can be simplified and made memorable;
(c) The audience – their age range, level of catering experience, their current job;
(d) How the course will be structured;
(e) If there will be any need for assessment; and
(f) If there will be any feedback/follow up required.

4 Newland Town Hall

Management Theme: Preparing A Competitive Tender Proposal

Introduction

Providing a good and cost-effective catering service is becoming more and more important. In order to increase productivity and efficiency, companies are being invited to tender, that is, to put forward a report on how they would operate/develop a catering service as well as to produce a financial appraisal outlining projected costs and profits.

Aims

To develop skill in producing a tender proposal which demonstrates a sound grasp of the situation and puts forward realistic and achievable proposals in a way that is attractive to the reader.

Competences Required for this Case

(a) Theoretical knowledge of the competitive tendering concept;
(b) Report writing skills; and
(c) Presentation skills.

Frances Jefferson took the lift down to her office on the second floor of Newland Town Hall, entered the door labelled 'Catering Manager' and went into the office of her assistant manager, John Dean.

John	Hello, Fran. How did the meeting go with the Catering Executive Committee?
Fran	If you mean did we get our budget increased, the answer is 'no'. In fact, at the moment, we have not even *got* a budget for next year.
John	What? That's impossible. What on earth are they doing to us?
Fran	Well, it appears that the decision has already been taken to put the Town Hall catering service out to competitive tender.
John	Oh, I see. I suppose we are all going to have to find other jobs.
Fran	No, John. At least not yet anyway. We have been asked to submit a tender as the 'in-house team'.
John	Well, we should do well. After all, we must know more about our set-up here than any outside contract company. I suppose it's just a process we have to go through to stay doing what we are doing anyway.
Fran	Not quite. If anything, we have got to improve our product and service. I have been given a briefing document from management which summarises the main points of the Town Hall's five-year plan. As a department we have been asked to produce a catering proposal for the future and to give a presentation to the Catering Executive Committee in six weeks' time.
John	Six weeks! That's no time. Who are the other companies?
Fran	I don't know. They would not reveal names. All they would say is that there are three other companies.
John	I'm beginning to get worried. How are we going to approach this?
Fran	Well it's 4 pm now and I still have a lot to do today before I go home. I suggest we think about it tonight and meet tomorrow at 8 am in my office to discuss our strategy.
John	Sounds fine to me. I'll give some thought to the matter tonight.

The next morning, Frances felt somewhat happier. She had spent the previous evening considering her plan of action and she realised that she was in a strong position. She had worked at the Town Hall for two years and knew the strengths and weaknesses of her department. Fran was in an optimistic mood that morning and was looking forward to discussing her ideas with John. In a way, both John and Fran saw the tender as a challenge which they were determined to win.

At the morning meeting Frances showed John a few notes which she had made the previous evening.

Tender proposals

1. Need to emphasis our strengths over the competition and to play down our weaknesses.
2. Need to look at the quality of our product and service and show how both of these could be improved.
3. Must show how productivity can be improved and costs reduced.
4. Need to increase the turnover and profitability.
5. Need to look at new sources of business and how we market ourselves.

Fran   These are just some first thoughts, John, but I thought we needed something on paper to help us plan our submission.

John   Absolutely Frances. I'm sure this is an excellent starting point. I too have given some thought to our approach and have written down the following.

John handed Frances his sheet of paper:

Areas to focus on for tender proposal

Finance – need to reduce costs and improve profitability
Product/Service – need to improve quality of both
Marketing – need to promote ourselves internally and externally.

> *Fran*   I like your approach, John. What I would like you to do now is to produce an outline for our proposal which we can use at our presentation. I will give you a copy of the tender document which you will need.

Frances handed John the competitive tender form and he agreed to work on producing the outline for the coming meeting. You are a graduate management trainee on industrial attachment, and John has asked you to help by producing a first draft.

NEWLAND TOWN HALL

COMPETITIVE TENDER FORM

Notes of Guidance for Applicants

The following notes of guidance have been prepared by the Executive Catering Committee in order to assist external organisations who have been invited to tender.

REQUIREMENTS

Whilst the Committee does not wish to dictate the presentation of each proposal it has requested that the following information be provided:

1.   Product Policy (for the short and long term)

2.   Staffing Policy (to include recruitment, retention and staff development)

3.   Quality Policy

4.   Financial Resources (whilst exact costings are not required at this stage, an indication of what capital expenditure would be advantageous.)

5.   Marketing Policy

6.   Equal Opportunities Policy

Background Information

Three hundred and fifty people currently work at Newland Town Hall. The catering facilities are twenty five years old and comprise a self-service cafeteria and a Management Dining Room which operates a silver-service style operation. Whilst the majority of the staff use the cafeteria for their morning coffee and afternoon tea breaks only 50% avail themselves of the cafeteria facilities at lunch time.

The menus work on a two-week cycle and offer a choice of starters, main courses and sweets. In general the catering facilities are understaffed at the mid-morning and afternoon breaks and overstaffed at lunch time.

With regard to cost effectiveness the new Council is committed to reducing costs and raising standards. The Committee will be particularly interested in receiving tender proposals that focus on increasing productivity and improving product quality.

The council is an equal opportunities employer. The Committee will wish to know about the tendering company's policy regarding staff training, pay and benefits and related personnel matters. Staff currently work a shift system.

Finally these notes have been developed to give potential contractors a guide to the areas which the Committee wish the initial presentation to focus on.

Warning

Canvassing any council official will lead to disqualification and termination of any existing contract with the council.

Points to be Considered when Dealing with this Case

To be successful in producing competitive tenders certain skills are needed. One of the key skills is the ability to present a comprehensive, informative and professional report.

In preparing your report you should consider the following:

(a) The underlying objectives of competitive tendering:

- Why has it been introduced?
- How does it work?
- Who is involved?
- What are the advantages and disadvantages of the process?

(b) The strengths and weaknesses of the 'in-house team':

- What experience do they have?
- What research are they likely to have undertaken?
- What is the current state of the catering operation?
- What difficulties have been incurred?
- What are the competing companies' strengths and weaknesses?

5 The String of Pearls

Management Theme: Controlling Stock

Introduction

Stock control is a very important aspect of a manager's job. There is a need to ensure that the correct levels of stock are maintained and that wastage does not occur as a result of poor stock control procedures.

Aims

To develop skills in identifying problems and their underlying causes, and proposing solutions.

Competences Required for this Case

(a) Theoretical knowledge of manual and computerised stock control systems;
(b) Ability to apply theoretical knowledge to practical problems; and
(c) Report writing skills.

The String of Pearls nightclub is situated in the heart of Manchester. It was opened twelve years ago by Frank Riley and Les Edwards. Although they had no direct experience of running a nightclub they had both worked in the leisure business for some twenty years. Les had been a bingo hall manager for the Gold Corporation and had worked all over the UK for them, while Frank had been an entertainments manager for Tropic Holiday Parcs in Scarborough and Blackpool.

They had both been born and brought up in Manchester and as friends at school had dreamed and talked about working together. They had stayed in contact over the years and at Les's forty-fifth birthday party they decided to start their own business. Les believed there was a need for a nightclub to serve both the local resident and business traveller markets.

Les and Frank looked at a number of sites before deciding to buy an old, disused community hall from the local authority with the aim of converting it into a nightclub. After spending a total of £250,000, including a loan from the bank, on purchasing and refurbishing the club they had a very attractive establishment. The club facilities consisted of a bar, a games room (with two snooker tables and a variety of fruit machines), a discotheque, a forty-seat restaurant with a carvery operation, and a bar snack area providing meals such as scampi in the basket, chicken nuggets and club sandwiches.

It had taken the club two years to break even and then for a number of years there had been a steady increase in both sales and profits. Last year, for the first time, the club's profits declined, but neither Frank nor Les could identify exactly what had brought this about. Their accountant believed that inefficient stock control was part of the problem and he suggested that a reappraisal of stock control procedures would be a good place to start.

Frank and Les took his advice. Andre Giovani had been their bar manager for the past seven years, and his head barperson, Ilesh Khan, had worked for the club for three years. They were both very different characters but had built up a good working relationship with Frank and Les. Andre tended to be a worrier and was very anxious when dealing with customers, whereas Ilesh was much more relaxed and was very popular with the regulars. Apart from Andre and Ilesh, the club employed six part-time bar staff. Ben, Lucy and Maria were students at the nearby university and they worked one evening a week each plus one Saturday night in three. During the Easter, Christmas and summer university vacations the club had to recruit extra labour, as the remaining part-time staff, Harry, Barbara and Wendy could not cope with the volume of business on their own. Harry had been a production worker at a local engineering firm but when it closed two years previously he had to take a job in a local supermarket. Unable to support his family on his wages, however, he regularly worked three nights a week at the club to earn extra money. Barbara and Wendy were both single parents who shared looking after their children and working alternate evenings at the club.

At the last audit there had been a discrepancy between the book figure and the stock figure. Frank had overlooked this because he knew that a number of clients had been given drinks as part of evening promotions. However, when Frank and Les asked for the next month's figures they noticed that the discrepancy between the book figure and the stocktake was getting bigger. Frank and Les knew that they could no longer regard the difference as a one-off occurrence and decided to carry out a full investigation.

Frank asked Andre if he could throw any light on the problem. Andre explained that he had no idea why his stock figures were low but was adamant that none of his staff were secret drinkers. He believed that he could sort the matter out if only he had more staff. Unfortunately, most of his time was spent serving and talking to customers and this inevitably made it nearly impossible for him to properly supervise his staff. Frank agreed to let him have one of the restaurant waiters transferred to bar duties as a full-time assistant while Andre reviewed the bar operations and accounted for the stock difference.

After the meeting with Frank, Andre went back to the bar, where he told Ilesh what had happened. Andre was very upset, as Frank had left him feeling that if he did not solve the problem he would be looking for another job. Ilesh calmed Andre, telling him that there must be a rational explanation and the way to find it was to draw a flow chart to show what happens to all stock movements. Andre agreed and during his lunch break he sketched out the following diagram:

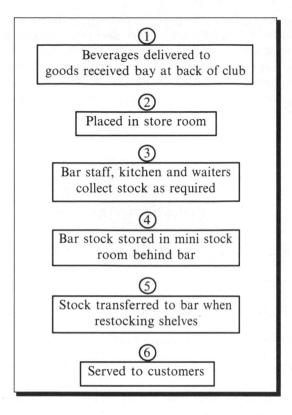

After lunch Andre, returned to the bar. Feeling happier, he showed his diagram to Ilesh.

Ilesh   Yes, you have made a start but this is not the whole story, is it?

Andre Well, I know we need a bit more detail but at least I have got something on paper. We must find an answer. Sometimes I think if I had done a management course it would help me with such matters.

Ilesh   Well, why don't you ask the new company trainee manager who has just joined the club. I heard him talking about some management project which he has got to write for the part-time management course he is doing. Perhaps he could make our stock control problem the focus of his study.

Andre Sounds a marvellous idea to me. I will speak to him tonight.

That night Andre explained the problem to George, the trainee manager. He said he would be glad to help if he could use the information as part of his in-company project. Andre agreed. George told Andre that his first task would be to draw up a checklist of points to help him identify how the current system operated, and agreed to start work immediately.

That week George designed a questionnaire and asked Andre to complete it.

CONFIDENTIAL

Bar Stock Questionnaire For The String Of Pearls

Section One

Procedure For Receiving Stock

1.1   Where are the goods unloaded? *At the back of the club; the door is next to the kitchen exit.*

1.2   How are the goods taken to the store room/cellar? *Sometimes by our storekeeper Fred and sometimes by the delivery people — if we are lucky!*

1.3   Who counts the stock in? *Depends who is around at the time.*

1.4   Are purchase specifications used? *We have not got these as such.*

Section Two

Storage Methods

2.1   Who puts the stock in the stores? *Fred or one of his helpers.*

2.2   Is it checked at this stage? *looked at but not counted.*

2.3   Is the stock kept at the correct temperature or does wastage occur?

This is a problem area — sometimes the temperature controls don't work.

2.4   How are individual items of stock recorded when received?

on bin cards.

Section Three

Issuing Procedures

3.1   When can stock be issued? *Anytime, as long as Fred is about to receive the requisitions*

3.2   What documents must be completed to obtain stock?

a requisition

3.3   Which members of the bar staff collect stock?

Anyone who has the time

3.4   Who signs the requisitions?

Me or a member of the bar staff.

3.5   Where does the stock go when it is issued?

To our mini store area at the back of the bar.

Section Four

Pricing of Issues

4.1   How is the stock priced from the stores? *We don't do that — we just note how many items*

4.2   Do you get regular reports from the stores on how much stock has been issued to you each week?

We do but they are always about six weeks behind; not all that useful by then.

Any Other Comments

It may be worth knowing that we also issue stock from the bar to the restaurant and kitchen. This is a headache sometimes as kitchen and bar staff don't always have a proper requisition form — but they usually produce one at some stage.

Please provide a diagram of your stores area in relation to the goods received bay and your bar plus the layout of your bar in relation to other areas e.g. restaurant, kitchen etc.

Thank you

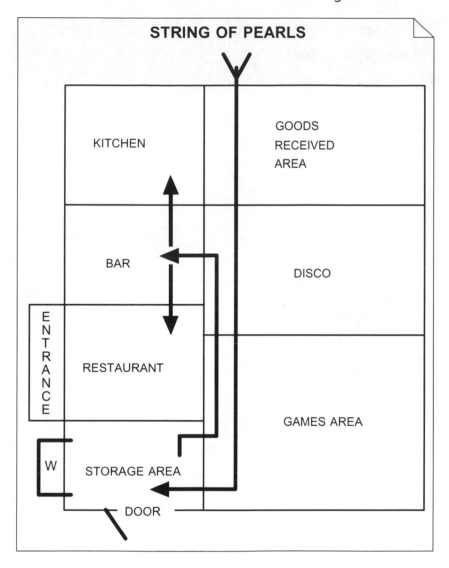

Having studied the questionnaire and Andre's diagram you have been asked to:

1. Produce a report for Andre outlining the areas where you think his problems are occurring.
2. Recommend action to improve the system.
3. Outline the advantages that could be gained by introducing a computerised stock control system.

Points to be Considered when Dealing with this Case

Stock is an important current asset of any company. It is a significant part of working capital, and effective stock control will increase the profitability of the business. Managers must, therefore, be diligent in their control of stock. To this end many organisations have moved towards the installation of a computerised system in order to gain greater efficiency in the management of their stock.

In answering the questions you should consider the following:

(a)   The objectives of a stock control system:

- Why they are necessary?
- What are the advantages of an efficient stock control system?

(b)   How a stock control/system functions:

- The documents involved.
- The security systems.
- The stock audit.

(c)   Factors (benefits and disadvantages), which should be taken into consideration when introducing and implementing a computerised system:

- Manpower.
- Time.
- Resources.
- Communication.
- Future expansion.

Part II
Front Office and Accommodation Management

6 Hamilton College of Further Education

Management Theme: Planning and Designing Accommodation

Introduction

The design of accommodation is becoming increasingly sophisticated. In order to ensure attractive and practical accommodation, certain design criteria need to be taken into consideration.

Aims

To develop skills in planning and designing new accommodation.

Competences Required for this Case

(a) Knowledge of design criteria;
(b) Application of knowledge to practical situations; and
(c) Techniques of interior design.

Hamilton College of Further Education is situated two miles south of the busy city of Colchester in Essex. The college is a ten-minute walk away from the main line railway station which operates a direct service to Liverpool Street in London.

The college was opened in 1962 by Sir Charles Archibald, a local businessman, who had a particular interest in the development of educational courses for local young people in science and technology. Since then, the college has developed to provide not only science and technology courses but also programmes in hospitality management, business studies, the media, and dance and drama. The college's director, Peter Wright, regularly refers to the college as a 'centre of excellence' when he speaks to his staff at their monthly meetings. His academic staff know that he has far-reaching plans to increase both the range of courses and the college's income.

On his appointment as director, Peter Wright decided to restructure the management team. A major feature of this exercise was the recruitment of Simon Wiseman as the new marketing director. Simon's first project was to develop new overseas markets. Peter Wright believed that if the college was to survive it had to recruit full-fee-paying overseas students to its courses.

Simon assured Peter that overseas students could be recruited but warned that residential accommodation would have to be built on the campus. At present, most students live within travelling distance of the college and while temporary accommodation could be provided, permanent residential facilities would have to be built.

At the last Governors' Meeting it was agreed that the college should approach a firm of architects to design a new residential block for the college, which could form the basis for a planning application.

You currently work as a consultant for the firm of architects specialising in the design of this type of accommodation. You have been asked to write a report outlining:

1. The design criteria that should be considered when planning the new accommodation block for the students.
2. The particular factors that should be considered to ensure the accommodation block is suitable for physically disabled students.

Points to be Considered when Dealing with this Case

The design of buildings has become very topical, given the current interest in environmental and architectural issues. Managers need to take into consideration certain design criteria and develop accommodation of a high standard that meets the expectations and needs of the market. In answering the questions you should consider the following:

(a) The needs of the users of the accommodation:

- Standard expected.
- Requirements.
- Flexibility needs.
- Degree of use.

(b) Trends in interior decoration and furnishings:

- Colour schemes.
- Textiles.
- Durability.
- Costs.
- Styles.
- Safety.

7 Countrywide Manors

Management Theme: Motivating Staff

Introduction:

Keeping staff motivated is a continuous challenge for management. In a sales environment it is particularly important that personnel are encouraged to improve on their previous performance, thereby increasing sales and profits.

Aims

To develop skills in creating original effective solutions to recurring problems.

Competences Required for this Case

(a) Knowledge of the main motivational theories;
(b) Report writing skills; and
(c) Ability to apply theoretical concepts to real-life situations and problems.

Rob Sharp sat thinking at his desk. Only two years before he had been delighted when the managing director of Countrywide Manors had given him approval to set up a central advanced reservations office at their head office in Oxford, but now he could not help wondering if it had been a mistake.

Countrywide Manors is a group of thirty country estates that have joined together to form a group marketing company. The group has gone from strength to strength over the past two years, marketing the manor houses to clients wishing to use the establishments for weddings, balls and garden parties.

Business was so successful that the group decided eighteen months ago to move into the corporate business market and offer the manor houses for company conferences, management training courses and new product launches also. Due to the increase in demand there have been a number of booking problems over the past fourteen months. In the main this has been caused by a lack of co-ordination with the booking offices in the thirty individual establishments; on some occasions the manor houses have been double booked. This has led to a high level of customer dissatisfaction, with some customers refusing to use Countrywide Manors again.

It was these problems which had led Rob Sharp as group marketing manager, to propose that the company set up a centralised booking service. He felt that there were a number of benefits to operating in this way, not least of which were:

1. Potential to maximise bookings in all thirty houses.
2. A better service for customers and potential customers.
3. Rationalisation of pricing policies.
4. Potential for group promotional campaigns.
5. Ability to use market research techniques on group customers.

The board of directors were in agreement with Rob's ideas and they approved his proposal to set up a central reservations team at head office. At the meeting it was agreed that Rob should contact Melissa Denby, the group personnel officer, to organise the recruitment of a central reservations team.

After some discussion, Rob and Melissa decided to advertise in the trade press for three advance reservation officers and one supervisor. The basic salary offered was to be between £8000 and £9250 and the supervisor was to be offered a salary in the range £8500 to £10,000 depending on age and experience.

Two months later the staff were in post. Sandra Roderick was the new advanced reservations supervisor; at the age of 39 she had three years' experience as a reservations clerk with Bookwell, a leading travel agent. Before that she had been a hotel receptionist for two years with the Excel Hotel Group. Julie Parsons, Suzanne Eldridge and Martin Cruise were recruited as the reservation officers. Both Julie and Suzanne were new to this type of work. Julie had worked for the past two years as a secretary for a local advertising agency and Suzanne had worked in the classified advertisement sales department for a local newspaper. Martin had just graduated and had been recruited by the company as one of their management trainees.

At first the reservation team worked well together. All four members of the department were pleased with their salaries and company benefits. During the first four months the team were enthusiastic and worked hard to bring in new business for the group. However, two months later, the number of advanced reservations began to decline. Rob Sharp decided to investigate the problem and obtained a computer printout.

Rob was amazed at the downward slope of the graph. He had expected the number of bookings to be slow in the first couple of months while clients were discovering the new service, but after that he had expected the central reservations system to bring about a large increase in business. As he was puzzling about the problem, Melissa Denby came into his office to talk about the high level of absenteeism in the new advance reservations department. Rob was very interested and told Melissa that he was concerned at the level of bookings being achieved by the central reservations team.

Melissa and Rob spent the next hour discussing what could be the cause of the problem. Overall, Melissa felt that the reservation team were becoming demotivated because of a lack of job satisfaction. At first Rob found this hard to believe. After all, the company was paying 10 per cent more than similar firms and their benefits package was one of the best in the industry. However, Rob agreed that something needed to be done and they agreed to look into the problem from a human resource management perspective. Melissa agreed to prepare a report for Rob on how the reservations team could be motivated, with particular reference to job design and productivity issues.

You are working as a management trainee in the personnel department and Melissa has asked you to write a draft report on staff motivation, with particular reference to the issues outlined.

Points to be Considered when Dealing with this Case

Applying motivational theories to the practice of human resource management is a complex task. There are a number of different theorists in this area – Maslow, Herzberg and McGregor are three of the major theorists discussed in most management theory texts. A highly motivated staff is an essential requirement for any hospitality organisation operating in an extremely competitive marketplace. In answering the questions you should consider the following:

(a) The basic concepts of established motivational theories:

- Reward systems.
- Job satisfaction.
- Working conditions.
- Self-development.

(b) How modern systems of work can encompass employee motivation techniques:

- Job design.
- Performance appraisal.
- Management by objectives.

8 Clevden Residential Management Centre

Management Theme: Decision-making

Introduction

Many large organisations are investing significant sums of money in training and developing their staff. In order to carry out this training a number of companies are purchasing small conference/training centres and operating their own courses.

Aims

To develop analytical and communication skills.

Competences Required for this Case

(a) Theoretical knowledge of factors to consider when selecting a location for a conference/training centre; and the benefits and disadvantages of building a new conference centre versus the conversion of an established centre;

(b) Theoretical knowledge of the factors to consider when designing conference facilities; and

(c) Presentation skills.

Clevden is a major UK food retailing company. For the last three years the firm has been investing heavily in training in an attempt to reduce the level of labour turnover amongst its junior and middle managers, and to increase the expertise of its senior managers and directors. Nick Blair, the company's personnel and training manager, has developed a series of one-week residential management development programmes which he operates in two local hotels through the spring and autumn months. Due to the success of these programmes, the managing director, George Grahams, has decided that the company should purchase a country house in which to run its courses. He sees it not only as a way of cutting training costs but also as a good investment. George has suggested to Nick that the management centre could be hired out to other companies during the winter and summer, when Clevden had limited use for it.

Nick has been to see local estate agents Huckle, Busby and Wolf, near Clevden's head office in Sheffield and has obtained details of a very interesting old manor house set in 24 acres of parkland. The house is close to the motorway network and only a short drive from the main line railway station.

At the last board meeting the purchase of a company training centre was discussed. While the directors are happy to invest the money, they have decided to seek professional advice from Q. A. Property Consultants. You work for Q. A. Property Consultants, and specialise in dealing with corporate property acquisitions, and have agreed to give a presentation to the Clevden directors on the following matters at their next board meeting.

1. What are the advantages of locating the training conference centre close to our head office? What factors should the company consider before deciding upon the location of the training centre?
2. The directors would like to know whether or not they should build a new conference centre or modify an existing old manor house.
3. They would like your advice on how the bedrooms, dining area and conference facilities should be designed to cater for delegate comfort and safety.

Points to be Considered when Dealing with this Case

Training is a key issue for any organisation. Companies have to make the decision to either send their staff on external courses or alternatively set up their own in-house training programmes. In the latter case, many companies are purchasing additional premises and setting up their own training centres. In answering the questions you should consider the following:

(a) Characteristics of a good location for a conference/ training centre.

(b) The advantages and disadvantages of converting an existing building or establishing a new centre:

- Financial implications.
- Client needs.
- Time available.
- Future plans.
- Technical considerations.

(c) Design requirements for the centre:

- Level of usage.
- Delegate profile.
- Availability of resources.
- Flexibility requirements.
- Durability.

9 The Lord Dubarry

Management Theme: Improving Communications

Introduction

The root cause of many organisational problems is poor communication. Managers need to ensure that communications are as effective as possible and that all staff realise the importance of team work and departmental co-operation.

Aims

To develop analytical and problem-solving skills.

Competences Required for this Case

(a) Ability to identify cause and effect; and
(b) Ability to develop solutions and plan their implementation.

As the market research assistant, based at the head office of the Star Group of hotels in Slough, Elliot O'Connor had been running a customer satisfaction survey for the past six months in the group's ten hotels. He had produced a questionnaire and sent it to all front office managers requesting them to ensure that every guest received a copy when they registered at their hotel. In order to encourage a good response rate, Elliot had arranged for each guest who completed a questionnaire to receive a Star keyring.

At the end of each month the questionnaires were sent to Elliot to be analysed. The hotel scoring the highest points was awarded a gold star and was sent a crate of champagne for its staff to enjoy. A certificate signed by the chairman of the group, Charles Coleman, was also sent to the hotel, to be displayed in the reception area.

Elliot had just received a printout of the survey results for the previous month. For the fifth time in succession the Clarence had come top. As it was the group's flagship hotel, Elliot was not surprised by this result. He scanned the rest of the details and then paused as he noticed that the Lord Dubarry had for the third month running come out badly in the ratings. Elliot obtained the following list of comments made most frequently by guests staying at the hotel.

THE STAR GROUP

Hotel Code Number: 1179/Lord Dubarry

Customer Survey Results: May

The following comments have been made by twenty or more customers staying in the hotel over the last month:

1.   Room not ready on arrival.

2.   Asked for item to be placed in bedroom e.g. cot, bedboard etc and it did not arrive until the Duty Manager was called for.

3.   Room given on arrival had not been cleaned. Customer had to ask for another room.

4.   Room Attendant did not know which day guest was leaving.

5.   Customer complained at Reception about a fault in the bedroom e.g. too hot, dripping tap and the fault was never rectified.

6.   Receptionist did not seem to know which rooms were vacant.

Elliot could see that there were problems in the front office and house-keeping departments of the Lord Dubarry so he decided to give a copy of the data to the operations manager, Paul Adams.

When Paul read the results he decided to alter his schedule for the next day. Instead of his planned routine inspection of the Majestic in Exeter he would make a surprise visit to the Lord Dubarry in Cambridge.

Paul left home very early to avoid the heavy traffic on the motorway and on arrival at the hotel asked the receptionist to tell the general manager, Richard Deacon, that he would like to see him. Minutes later Richard was in Reception greeting Paul.

Richard	Well, Paul, this is a pleasant surprise. What can we do for you?
Paul	It's not so much what you can do for me, but rather what I can do for you.
Richard	This sounds intriguing. Why don't you join me for breakfast in the coffee shop and we'll have a chat.
Paul	I was hoping you would suggest that Richard. I've been on the road since 6 am and I could do with one of your good English breakfasts.
Richard	Now, Paul, tell me why you have come to see me?
Paul	Well, I won't beat about the bush. I have been looking through the customer questionnaires from your hotel and quite frankly, Richard, there are serious implications for your front office and housekeeping departments.
Richard	Oh no. What have the customers been saying?
Paul	Look. I've brought you a copy.
Richard	I knew there were difficulties in the accommodation area but I never realised the extent of them. Something must be done immediately.
Paul	Yes. The question is, what do you propose to do, and how can we at head office help you?
Richard	I need a week to discuss the matter with my front office manager and head housekeeper. Then I'll come back to you and let you know my proposals.
Paul	Yes, that sounds all right but don't be at the bottom of the list again this month, as the managing director is not pleased with your hotel's performance at the moment.

After Paul had said goodbye to Richard he returned to his office and telephoned Diana Barnes, his front office manager, and Shirley Maples, his head housekeeper. He asked them to meet him in his office at 2 pm that afternoon.

The meeting started promptly. Richard began the meeting by telling Diana and Shirley about the visit and the problems which Paul had brought to his attention.

Richard	As you can see, the list of complaints is concerned with your two departments. I thought it would be a good idea for the three of us to work out together how these problems are arising.
Diana	I must admit this does not come as a complete surprise to me. For the last couple of months there seems to have been a growing tension between my staff and the staff in the housekeeping department.
Richard	How do you feel about this, Shirley? Have you noticed any difficulties between front office staff and the staff in the housekeeping department.
Shirley	No, not really, although I don't have that much contact with my room attendants. It's the floor housekeepers who see them the most.
Richard	We must develop a strategy for overcoming this problem. I've got to report to Paul next week with our proposals for improving customer service.
Diana	My suggestion is that at my weekly meeting with the front office staff I will explain the comments we have received from some of the customers and ask if they can indicate why these difficulties have occurred. If you can do the same, Shirley, then we can all meet again and decide what action we should take.
Richard	I like your suggestion, Shirley, what do you think?
Shirley	Yes, I'll do what I can, but I can't promise you that my staff will contribute much.

A week later Richard, Diana and Shirley met to discuss the results of the meeting with the front office and housekeeping staff.

Richard	How did your two meetings go?
Shirley	Not very well, I'm afraid, Richard. My staff felt they were being blamed for the problems and since the meeting one of them has resigned.

Diana	Are you implying that it's my staff who are at fault?
Shirley	I think that's for you to decide.
Diana	Just because you find it difficult to work with some of your staff I suppose you think you'll blame my department. Well, let me tell you I have an excellent team who are committed to the hotel. I only wish I could say the same for your staff.
Richard	Stop this. Its not solving anything, but it does highlight the scale of the communication problem between your two departments. I am going to ask head office to send someone down from operations division to take an impartial view on what is happening and see if they can advise us.

You work in the operations department at head office of the Star group and have received the following memo from your Manager Paul Adams:

STAR GROUP

MEMORANDUM

To: Operations Development Officer

From: Operations Manager

Please can you take a look at the following comments made about the Lord Dubarry. See Elliott in market research if you need any more information. Richard Deacon would like the information as soon as possible so can you let me have your report by the end of the week, outlining:

1.   Why you think these communication problems are occurring?

2.   How the communication problems can be overcome?

Points to be Considered when Dealing with this Case

Communication is an ongoing activity in any organisation. For many companies there are problems in this area. Managers need to be able to recognise the signs of ineffective communication at all levels in the organisation and develop strategies to overcome them. In answering the questions you should consider the following:

(a)   The types of communication which takes place in any organisation:

- Written.
- Verbal.
- Visual.

(b)   The range of communication problems:

- Misinterpretation.
- Avoidance.
- Misunderstanding.
- Lack of co-operation.

(c)   Underlying causes of communication problems.

- Why people communicate ineffectively.
- Time.
- Resources.
- Personalities.

(d)   Techniques for dealing with the problems:

- People.
- Technology.

10 The Dunadry

Management Theme: Introducing New Technology

Introduction

New technology is being introduced rapidly to hospitality organisations, especially in the front office area. Managers must assess the benefits to be gained from computerisation and develop a plan for successful implementation.

Aims

To develop evaluative and judgemental skills.

Competences Required for this Case

(a) Theoretical knowledge of computer systems and their application to the front office area; and

(b) Ability to apply theory to practice with regard to the implementation of the change process.

Michael O' Reilly joined the Unicorn group as one of their graduate management trainees eleven years ago. He is now 31 and already a member of the company's senior management team having just been appointed as general manager of the Dunadry Hotel.

On his appointment, the managing director had given Michael the brief to update the hotel's systems and human resources. Michael knew this was going to be a difficult task: many of the staff had been with the hotel for a long time and they took pride in the way it was run. The previous manager, Joseph O'Leary, had often boasted to staff and customers alike that his old-fashioned methods worked best. Although his methods had not always pleased the company's directors, he had been popular with both staff and customers.

Michael knew that this made his mission all the more difficult and decided to approach the matter by dividing his tasks into three main areas:

> 1. Food and beverage operations.
> 2. Front office and accommodation operations.
> 3. Managerial functions (marketing, personnel, purchasing and accounts).

Joseph O' Leary disliked computers and had refused to use them in the hotel: Michael's first task was to computerise the front office department. He planned to computerise the other areas later. Michael knew that in order to introduce any change in this area he would have to appoint a new member of staff who understood computers.

You are one of the applicants for the post of systems manager, and have been asked to give a presentation outlining:

> 1. The possible applications of a computer in the front office area.
> 2. The benefits of computerising the front office.
> 3. How to involve staff in the change process.
> 4. How the benefits of computerisation can be explained to the hotel's guests, who like the old system.

Points to be Considered When Dealing with this Case

Computers have a number of applications in the front office department. Advance reservations control, registration, billing and cashiering are the main areas in which new technology usually features. Given the pace of change with regard to technology, managers need to keep up to date with new applications and their benefits to ensure their organisation has the competitive edge. In answering the questions you should consider the following:

(a) The basic components of a computer system:

- The hardware.
- The software.

(b) The benefits of a computer system to:

- The organisation.
- The guest.
- The management.
- The staff.

(c) The implementation of a computer system:

- Who should be involved?
- Time scale.
- The conversion process from the old to the new system.

Part III

Human Resources Management

11 The Grand Hotel

Management Theme: Management Recruitment

Introduction

In today's hospitality industry it is becoming increasingly important that the right people are recruited into management positions. Organisations cannot afford to make mistakes in this area. As a result, many hospitality companies are working to improve the effectiveness of their recruitment processes.

Aims

To develop evaluative and judgemental skills.

Competences Required for this Case

(a) Theoretical knowledge of management recruitment methods;

(b) Ability to analyse and evaluate curricula vitae; and

(c) Implementation of appropriate selection methods.

As the general manager of the Grand Hotel, a 5-star luxury hotel in the centre of Paris, you need to recruit a new front of house manager to replace Geraldine Dickens whom you have promoted to deputy general manager. You have decided to engage the services of a well-established management selection agency – Hale and Scott – to carry out the first step in the selection process.

Pamela Scott, the director, has today sent you a copy of the advertisement, together with three of the most promising CVs they have received, for your consideration.

Hale and Scott
Leaders in Management Recruitment for the Hospitality Industry

Senior Front of House Manager — Paris
Salary circa £20,000 + Benefits

We are recruiting on behalf of a leading international hotel chain for a Senior Front of House Manager to work in their flagship hotel which is located in the centre of Paris.

You will probably be in your late thirties with experience of working in a first-class hotel. You must possess the drive, energy and enthusiasm to manage and motivate your staff whilst at the same time creating an efficient and friendly customer environment.

You will be fluent in French and ideally one other major European language and hold a recognised qualification in hospitality management.

Initial enquires and CV should be addressed to:

Pamala Scott
Director of Recruitment
Hale and Scott
PO Box 217
London. WC1 2RC

Illustration reproduced with the kind permission of the Hilton International

Curriculum Vitae

Personal Details

Surname: Pringle   Forenames: Felicity Jane

Marital Status: Divorced with two children – Pippa (9)
                 and Jeremy (7).

Age: 37   Date of Birth: 1/8/54

Place of Birth: Richmond, England

Home Address: 12 Lakeside Way, Marlow, Bucks MB3 5XJ

Telephone No: (06285) 1947

Education and Qualifications

Stansfield High School for Girls, Kew 1965–72

6 'O' Levels: English, French, History, Art, Biology, Maths

1 'A' Level: English

Other Achievements: Captain of school hockey team and sixth form prefect.

West London Polytechnic, 1972–75

HND Hotel Catering and Institutional Management
Awarded student of the year prize by Grandlux Hotels in 1974

Experience

The Amberley Country Club Hotel, Christchurch, Bournemouth
March–September 1974, industrial placement.

The International Hotel, Heathrow, London (600 beds)
September 1975–November 1976, Trainee Manager
The training period covered the following departments:
Front office, housekeeping, restaurant, bar, kitchen, personnel and accounts.

Le Hotel Internationale, Paris (200 beds)
December 1976–January 1978, Assistant Front Office Manager.
The job involved responsibility for six staff and in particular the introduction
of a new computerised reservations system.

Marlow Hospital, Bucks, March 1978–October 1980, Accommodation
Manager.
The job involved responsibility for a departmental budget of £250,000, the
recruitment and training of staff, setting and maintenance of standards,
purchasing and financial control.

October 1980–May 1987 – raising family.

During this period I worked for the Leisure Time Group as a part-time
consultant training their new front office staff for their luxury holiday
centres.

May 1987 to present – The Grand Hotel, Eastbourne, Front Office Manager.
Responsible for the day-to-day running of the department, recruiting and
training staff, budgetary control and generating sales.

Hobbies

Horseriding and tennis.

Curriculum Vitae

Current Employment

Front Office Manager, City Tower Hotel, Birmingham, England.

Name: Jason Howard   Age: 38   Place of Birth: France

Home Address: 3 The Grove, Kenton, Harrow, Middlesex

Experience and Education:

Front Office Manager at the City Tower since April 1984. The hotel is
family-owned and has 68 bedrooms. Although my job title is Front Office
Manager I am also responsible for the accommodation services.

From February 1980 to June 1983 (from June 1983 to March 1984 I was
in hospital). I was Head of Reservations at the Seaway Hotel in
Blackpool. I was responsible for maximising occupancy as well as being
involved in marketing the hotel. I also acted as Duty Manager.

I was Head Receptionist at the International Hotel in London between
November 1976 and February 1980 and as such gained good experience
of working in a large international hotel (600 bedrooms). I had
responsibility for training new staff, reservations, reception and
cashiering.

From July 1973 to October 1976 I was a Trainee Front Of House
Manager with the Majestic Group and worked in Windsor, Leeds and
Somerset.

My first job after graduating from college with a Hotel and Catering
Diploma (from the Hotel School in Lausanne) was with a family run
hotel in Switzerland.

Interests: cooking, sailing and golf.

Referee:
Mrs Jenkins
Manager
The Seaway Hotel, Branksome Way
Blackpool

Curriculum Vitae

Name: Mr Basit Shah Age: 47 years Nationality: British

Current Job: Room Sales Manager, Royal Gardens Hotel, Leicester

Background

1964–1966 – worked for T.Y.K. Hotels as a Trainee Manager in Oxford, Heathrow and Bordeaux, France.

October 1966–June 1969 BA degree at the International Management University, Geneva. Specialist options: Front Office and Accommodation Management.

January 1971–March 1973 – Worked for T.Y.K. Hotels as an Assistant Front Office Manager in Reading. I was responsible for the management of three staff; in December 1971 my abilities were recognised and I was promoted to take charge of reservations work where I stayed until I left in March 1973.

March 1973–May 1985 – Returned to India to help my father set up a new hotel/leisure complex. I then set up my own hotel but decided to return to England in 1985.

June 1985–present – Front Office Room Sales Manager at the Royal Garden Hotel. I have a team of eight staff and am responsible for financial planning, budgeting, pricing, and selling accommodation and conference facilities.

Since September 1987 I have been studying part-time for an M.B.A. at The Polytechnic of the Midlands.

Outside Interests:

Travelling and music

Referee

Mr E Abdul
General Manager
Royal Garden Hotel
Ferrymead High Road
Leicester
LN3 71J

Prepare a presentation using the case questions:

1. Why are employment consultants appointed by companies? What are the advantages and disadvantages of this method of recruitment?
2. To what extent do you feel the advertisement meets the need of the general manager in filling this post?
3. From the CVs, what would you consider to be the strengths and weaknesses of each candidate? What are the advantages and disadvantages of CVs as opposed to application forms?
4. What selection methods would you implement to choose the most appropriate candidate for this post?

Points to be Considered when Dealing with this Case

Employment consultants are often appointed to assist companies when recruiting management staff. In answering the first question, you should consider the following:

(a)   The role of employment consultants:

- How do they function?
- What are the financial implications?
- What expertise do they have?

(b)   In looking at Question 2, you should explore:

- the purpose(s) of advertising vacancies in the press; and
- the factors which must be considered when designing such advertisements.

(c)   Gathering information about applicants is a significant part of the recruitment process. In reviewing the pros and cons of curricula vitae as opposed to application forms you should consider the following issues:

- cost implications;
- administrative effort; and
- comparison of candidates.

continued opposite

(d)   When analysing each particular CV you should reflect on:

- the requirements of the management vacancy; and
- the suitability of each applicant in terms of:
    - qualifications;
    - experience;
    - enthusiasm for the post; and
    - potential to fit into current management team.

Finally, when answering Question 4, consider the range of selection methods available and decide the most appropriate method(s) for choosing the right person for the job. In making your decision, evaluate the extent to which the selection method allows the candidate to demonstrate:

- ability to work as a member of a team;
- problem-solving skills;
- interpersonal skills; and
- communication skills.

12   The Carlton Hotel

Management Theme: Appraising Employee Performance

Introduction

Formally appraising the performance of employees has been introduced into most large organisations over the past few years. However, quite often very little training or advice is provided for the appraisers or the appraisees on how to deal effectively with appraisal interviews.

Aims

To develop judgemental skills.

Competences Required for this case

(a)   Theoretical knowledge of appraisal systems.
(b)   Ability to analyse and interpret information.
(c)   Interview techniques.

As the executive head housekeeper of the Carlton Hotel in Birmingham, you have long been suggesting at your weekly management meetings with the general manager and the other heads of department that action should be taken to improve employee performance in the hotel. In the short time you have been with the organisation you have identified poor standards of service and low productivity as well as poor staff morale.

The general manager has decided to take up your suggestion and she asks you to chair a small working party to investigate the matter further and put forward recommendations to the next meeting of the board of directors. The IEP (Improving Employee Performance) group met three times, after which they produced a report and presented it to the next board meeting. The main recommendation was that a system of employee appraisal should be developed and implemented in the hotel. Whilst the board fully accepted the report's proposals they suggested that the appraisal system should first be tried out on a pilot basis. With the feedback from this exercise, they would then make a final decision as to whether or not they should accept the system for all the staff in the hotel.

As you had chaired the working party and been the originator of the project, the general manager has recommended that the housekeeping department should be used for the pilot exercise.

The Carlton Hotel

MEMORANDUM

To: The Executive Head Housekeeper

From: Personnel Manager

Subject: Appraisals

Please find attached the appraisal forms for your department. Please return the completed forms to me by the end of next month.

Thanks

Jenny

It is Monday morning and you have just received the above memo from Jenny Hartley the personnel manager, along with a batch of forms. You are rather surprised that Jenny is just expecting you to carry out the appraisals without any assistance or training from the personnel department. However, you do not really want to ask for her help, as she did not react very positively to the project in the first place.

You have decided that your first step will be to discuss the matter with your deputy executive head housekeeper and the floor housekeepers at the Wednesday afternoon departmental meeting. To explain what is involved in an employee appraisal system you have organised a small training session for them during the following week. Meanwhile, you have decided that the forms will be distributed to all the staff after the Wednesday meeting and they will then have ten days to complete their part of the form.

*   *   *

It is now five days since you circulated the appraisal forms to all your staff and you have received three completed forms. You decide to interview these three members of staff the following week. Their profiles, and the three completed review forms, are set out below.

Staff Profile 1

NAME: Jeremy Peter Reynolds

JOB TITLE: Deputy executive head housekeeper

CAREER PROFILE
Jeremy has a BA degree in Hotel Catering and Institutional Management from the Mid West Polytechnic. He graduated two years ago and has worked at the Carlton for eighteen months. Before this he spent six months with a country club hotel but he decided he was not suited to their style of operation.

During his initial probationary period Jeremy worked as a floor housekeeper and then just over a year ago he was promoted to become the deputy executive head housekeeper. The hotel has suffered from an extremely high level of labour turnover in the accommodation department and as a result Jeremy was offered the position which he now holds.

EMPLOYEE PERFORMANCE
Jeremy is a hard working individual who is highly motivated and ambitious. At twenty-three he has done well to reach his present managerial position with this hotel group.

In his enthusiasm to do his job well Jeremy has on a number of occasions found himself in conflict with the floor housekeepers.

As a result, the executive head housekeeper has had to intervene to resolve the problems. Most of the conflict appears to stem from the fact that Jeremy has a rather autocratic style of leadership and that he expects the staff to put as many hours as he does into the job.

Staff Profile 2

NAME: Daphne Belinda Mitchell

JOB TITLE: Senior floor housekeeper

CAREER PROFILE
Daphne has worked for the hotel for ten years during which time she has risen from being a room attendant to her present position. She was appointed to this post last year, at the age of 38, as a result of the re-organisation of the department.

EMPLOYEE PERFORMANCE
Whilst Daphne is excellent technically, she is not so strong in training new members of staff to meet her standards. Having been a room attendant and floor housekeeper in the hotel, Daphne feels she is the most qualified person to carry out the training of new staff. Jeremy Reynolds told her recently that she should become a qualified trainer. This led to a rather heated debate after which Daphne was determined to avoid going on any further training courses. She is obviously not comfortable in her new role and she needs some help.

STAFF PROFILE 3

NAME: Hazel Jane Gibbons

JOB TITLE: Floor housekeeper

CAREER PROFILE
Hazel has been a floor housekeeper with the hotel for three years. She joined after obtaining her BTEC National Diploma in Hotel and Catering Operations from the local college.

EMPLOYEE PERFORMANCE
Hazel has been a very good member of staff, but just lately she does not seem to be enjoying her work. Some of her room attendants have indicated that she has not been doing her job properly. In the reorganisation last year Hazel was not promoted and as a result was upset, especially as Jeremy had received rapid promotion.

Staff Performance Review   CONFIDENTIAL

Surname:.....*Reynolds*.......................... Initials:....*J.P.*....

Part 1
To be completed by the member of staff with reference to the job description.

1. Give a brief description of your main activities during the year. What do you consider are your most important responsibilities?

As the deputy executive head housekeeper I am responsible for overseeing the work of the floor house keepers — telling them the best way to carry out their duties and checking that they carry them out correctly. I assist the executive head housekeeper with budgeting, recruiting, producing staff rotas, checking on standards.

2. Describe your achievements and the contribution you have made during the year.

(a) Developed a procedures manual for the floor house keepers to follow.

(b) Developed a comprehensive training programme for all new members of staff.

(c) Altered the hours worked by floor housekeepers - enabling the department to work with one less member of staff and therefore reduce labour costs

3. State any difficulties you have had doing your job or in meeting your agreed objectives and suggest how these could be prevented or remedied.

(a) The main difficulty encountered has been getting the staff to work hard - they need to be 'chased' most of the time.

(b) My objective has been to try and raise the standard of our accommodation but this has been difficult due to low staff morale and a high level of absenteeism and labour turnover.

(c) With more discipline and measurement/monitoring of performance these problems could be reduced.

4. Do you consider that your present job fully utilises your abilities? If not, which of your abilities could be more fully utilised and how would your job need to be changed to accomplish this?

I don't feel the job currently fulfils me. I feel I could do more, especially on the management side of the department. I would like to carry out more of the staff management activities e.g. recruitment, training, discipline etc.

5. Briefly describe your career aspirations.

Basically, I would like to be an executive head housekeeper and then eventually a general manager.

When you have completed Part 1, please hand this form to your reporting officer.

Staff Performance Review   CONFIDENTIAL

Surname:...Mitchell.......................... Initials:...D. B....

Part 1
To be completed by the member of staff with reference to the
job description.

1. Give a brief description of your main activities during the
    year. What do you consider are your most important
    responsibilities?

    This has been my first year as senior
    floor housekeeper. During the year I
    have helped to train the new housekeepers
    during their induction period and have
    set up my own training programme for
    new room attendants

2. Describe your achievements and the contribution you have
    made during the year.

    My main achievements have been in
    training staff to attain a higher
    standard of work.
    I have also become involved in the
    selection process for the new room
    attendants and floor housekeepers.

3. State any difficulties you have had doing your job or in
    meeting your agreed objectives and suggest how these
    could be prevented or remedied.

    Sometimes I feel that my job
    overlaps somewhat with that of the
    deputy executive housekeeper –
    especially with regard to training
    new staff. I feel this should be
    left to me to do.

4. Do you consider that your present job fully utilises your abilities? If not, which of your abilities could be more fully utilised and how would your job need to be changed to accomplish this?

I enjoy training new staff when I am allowed to do things my way. At the moment I feel my job utilises my abilities.

5. Briefly describe your career aspirations.

To one day become a deputy executive head housekeeper.

When you have completed Part 1, please hand this form to your reporting officer.

Staff Performance Review   CONFIDENTIAL

Surname:......Gibbons.................   Initials:....H.G....

Part 1
To be completed by the member of staff with reference to the job description.

1. Give a brief description of your main activities during the year. What do you consider are your most important responsibilities?

(a) Organising room attendants
(b) Checking rooms
(c) Helping with the refurbishment of six rooms on my floor — discussing colour schemes, furnishings, etc. With the executive head housekeeper.

2. Describe your achievements and the contribution you have made during the year.

My achievements have been much the same as the past three years.

3. State any difficulties you have had doing your job or in meeting your agreed objectives and suggest how these could be prevented or remedied.

The job has become very routine.

4. Do you consider that your present job fully utilises your abilities? If not, which of your abilities could be more fully utilised and how would your job need to be changed to accomplish this?

No I would like to take on more responsibility.

5. Briefly describe your career aspirations.

To become an executive head housekeeper eventually.

When you have completed Part 1, please hand this form to your reporting officer.

Questions for this Case:

1. Draw up a check-list of points that the executive head housekeeper could use as a basis of the training session with the deputy and floor housekeepers.
2. How would you approach each of the appraisal interviews with Jeremy, Daphne and Hazel?
3. What goals would you wish to set each of the appraisees for the following year?
4. What support should be offered to each of the appraisees to help them achieve their objectives?

Points to be Considered when Dealing with this Case

Employee performance appraisal is an important element of human resource management. The process provides an opportunity for the appraisee to discuss the job he or she is doing, and any difficulties encountered in fulfilling their tasks. It is a two-way exchange and provides an opportunity for the past to be reflected upon and the future anticipated in terms of organisational and individual needs. In answering the questions you should consider the following:

(a) The objectives of employee performance appraisal:

- At the individual level.
- At the organisational level.

(b) The appraisal interview:

- Preparation required.
- Approach.
- Objectives.
- Follow-up.

(c) Training required:

- Interview techniques.
- Identification of training needs.

13 Inn on the Lake

Management Theme: Dealing with Staff Stress and Controlling Labour Turnover

Introduction

Stress at work is a key issue facing hospitality organisations, as very often staff work under the dual pressures of time and a heavy workload.

Aims

To develop skills in dealing with difficult situations and empathising with staff.

Competences Required for this case

(a) Theoretical knowledge of stress and its causes;
(b) Theoretical knowledge of labour turnover and its causes; and
(c) Ability to interpret situations and apply theory to practice.

It's Thursday afternoon and Imresh Patel the personnel manager, is working at his desk. Suddenly there is a knock at the door and Gary Saunders, the food and beverage manager, storms into the room.

Gary	It's no good, Imresh, I just can't go on! Sometimes I think this place is a madhouse. How can I manage when I don't have the staff? All the customers will be complaining and I can't say I blame them if there is no food for dinner.
Imresh	Calm down Gary. What's the problem?
Gary	Chefs! That's the problem. Even when they have the finest equipment they do nothing but complain. I wish we could operate without them by using robots as they do in the car factories.
Imresh	Well, you know how they are. If flash point occurs in the kitchen and they think that you are interfering you always run the risk of melt-down. Is that what's been happening?
Gary	No it's worse than that. I haven't been near the kitchens today – I've been far too busy. That is probably part of the problem. Anyway, Jean has just resigned, which means that the hotel has now lost three chefs in as many weeks. I've spoken to the agency and they have told me that they can provide relief cover at 30 per cent above their normal rates because of the lack of notice. I've accepted but something will have to be done.
Imresh	Has Jean left, or is he still on the premises?
Gary	Oh, he's still here. To calm him down Julie gave him a drink. The trouble is, he then took the bottle and is now a bit the worse for it.
Imresh	Ask him to come to my office. I'm not taking sides but I need to know why we are losing all our chefs. Then perhaps we can work out a solution to the problem. Leave it with me. Just remember, Gary, come Saturday morning, you'll be on holiday in Spain. Just take it easy. After all, we've had no customer complaints yet, so things could be worse.

Gary leaves. A few minutes later there is another knock at the door and in walks Jean.

Imresh	Come in and take a seat. I know you've just resigned but I would like a few words with you. I need to know why you have only been with us such a short time.
Jean	Look, I know I have been drinking but I'm amazed that I took the job. Long hours at low pay do not lead to happy staff. Also, I have no experienced kitchen assistants. Some of my assistants have just left school. No one seems to have thought of training them. They can hardly hold a knife let alone prepare vegetables. I was ending up doing everything myself and when the Salamander stopped working for the second time this week I just could not stand it any more. I'm going back to France, where the chef is treated with respect and has good equipment, before I become an alcoholic because of all the stress I've suffered here.

Questions for this Case:

1. Why is it important that managers understand stress?
2. What could be done to reduce the level of stress for chefs working in the hotel?
3. What other factors may have led to the high turnover of chefs in the hotel?

Points to be Considered when Dealing with this Case

Increasing pressures in the work environment have lead to high levels of stress being experienced by members of staff in many organisations. Managers need to understand how stress develops, be able to recognise the signs and be able to develop strategies to reduce stress levels. In answering the questions you should consider the following:

(a) How stress at work develops:

- The characteristics of the work.
- Relationships with colleagues.

(b) Recognising the symptoms:

- Physical signs of stress.
- Mental signs of stress.

(c) Dealing with stress:

- At the organisational level.
- At the employee level.
- How to reduce employee stress.

(d) Reasons for high levels of labour turnover:

- Financial implications.
- Productivity.
- Profitability.
- Employee morale.

14 The Valley View Hotel

Management Theme: Organisational Change

Introduction

Planning and implementing organisational change is a complex management task. Hospitality managers must develop strategies and introduce and implement change effectively in their operations.

Aims

To develop skills in dealing with difficult situations.

Competences Required for this Case

(a) Theoretical knowledge of organisational change issues.
(b) Ability to apply theory to practice with regard to the implication of the change process.

Hywel Davies walked out of the general manager's office knowing that at the end of the month, when the current assistant manager retired, he would become the next assistant manager of The Valley View Hotel. Hywel made his way back to his office on the third floor, where he poured himself a cup of coffee and sat for five minutes reflecting on his success. He was only twenty-three years old and this was his first job after graduating from the Mid-Wales Polytechnic three years before with a BA degree in Hospitality Management. Since starting as a management trainee he had progressed to become first the assistant front office manager and then, only fourteen months ago, front office manager. Hywel was particularly pleased with himself, as he had beaten his rival, David Jenkins, to the post even though David was the food and beverage manager and had been with the hotel for five years. He was not as innovative as Hywel but he was very hard-working, was well respected by members of his department and had long felt that the assistant manager's job would be his one day.

Hywel realised that he had an important challenge ahead of him as assistant manager. The Valley view was an attractive 50-bedroom hotel set in five acres of grounds, with an outdoor swimming pool and two tennis courts. The hotel had been managed by the Penhurst family for the past ten years; Thomas Penhurst was general manager and his brother, Ralph, assistant manager. But Thomas Penhurst realised that new, younger blood was needed to manage the hotel, as it was facing changing times. There had been a decline in sales over the past two years and a new hotel was about to be built only five miles away.

Thomas Penhurst realised that the hotel's management must develop a long-term strategy and he had asked Hywel to work on a sales action plan for the hotel.

Hywel set about the task of formulating the action plan. He decided to produce his own, as time was limited. He told his assistant, Gwen, that he was not to be interrupted except for emergencies, and shut himself in his office for three weeks. He emerged triumphant with a 40-page document on how every department and each member of staff could improve sales turnover in the coming year. The report was circulated to all heads of departments, together with a copy of the following questionnaire.

The Valley View Hotel
Sales Action Plan Questionnaire

As you know, I have been appointed the next Assistant Manager of this hotel. Our General Manager, Mr Penhurst, has asked me to develop a new strategy to improve sales turnover in the next five years. As it is the responsibliity of all of us to increase sales I thought you would like to have a look at the plan I have produced. As time is of the essence I would be grateful if you could complete the following questions and return the completed form to me by the end of the week.

1.   As a Head of Department at Valley View, how do you plan to implement the recommendations in the Action Plan for your department?
2.   What extra resources do you think you might need to meet your sales targets?
3.   Are there any additions that you would like to see made to the methods of improving sales? If there are, please list them.

Hywel Davies

Hywel Davies

Hywel circulated the sales action plan on a Monday morning and was expecting replies by Friday. But instead of the replies to his questionnaire, Hywel received a curt call from Mr Penhurst summoning him to his office immediately. Hywel leapt to his feet and ran upstairs to the fifth floor where he found a very angry general manager.

Mr Penhurst	I'm sure I don't need to tell you why I have called you into my office, Hywel. I must say it shows a remarkable management flair to be able to upset all of my departmental heads in just four weeks.
Hywel	I'm sorry. I don't know what you're talking about. Is it something to do with the new college trainee that I have given the 'improving productivity' project to?
Mr Penhurst	No, it certainly is not that, but I must say that I don't like the sound of that either. As you seem to have no clue as to why you are here let me explain. I asked you to develop some ideas for improving sales turnover. What I didn't want you to do was to upset all my heads of department with two of them offering me their resignations this morning.
Hywel	Well, if David Jenkins is one of them I would be tempted to accept, if you don't mind my saying so, Mr Penhurst. He seems to be upset since my promotion. I think he is jealous.
Mr Penhurst	When I want your opinions on staffing matters I will ask for them. At the moment, if anyone should be resigning it should be you. Look, I know you meant well but you have gone about the task wrongly. I have not got time to go through where you have gone wrong with this project, but what I have done is employ an outside consultant to advise you where you have made mistakes and to help you develop a more satisfactory result. Please see my secretary, on your way out and she will give you the consultant's name and telephone number. I want you to set up an appointment as soon as possible and I want to be involved at this meeting.

You have been appointed as the consultant to help Hywel. You have received a copy of the sales action plan and have been told by Thomas Penhurst how the plan had been produced and circulated with the questionnaire. You have also been told of the uproar this caused amongst the heads of department. You will be meeting Hywel for the first time tomorrow.

---

1. Draw up a list of points regarding the management of change that you want to discuss with him with reference to the way he developed his plan. Indicate why you think he upset everyone.
2. Draw up a new strategy for developing a revised action plan.

Points to be Considered when Dealing with this Case

Organisational change is an important issue facing hospitality managers. As the pace for change increases, managers need to plan changes carefully in order to increase their chances of success. In answering the questions you should consider the following:

(a)   The effects of organisational change in terms of:

- Human resources.
- Methods of work.
- Reward systems.
- Customer service.

(b)   Staff reactions to organisational change:

- Why people sometimes dislike change.
- How staff may respond to change.
- The effects on the organisation.

(c)   Implementing change effectively:

- Preparing staff.
- Providing resources.
- Developing support systems.

15 Kirby Lodge

Management Theme: Improving Standards

Introduction

In an increasingly competitive marketplace, today's hospitality manager must ensure that consistently high standards are established and maintained.

Aims

To develop analytical and problem-solving skills.

Competences Required for this Case

(a) Theoretical knowledge of quality circles;
(b) The application of knowledge to practical management problems; and
(c) The managerial techniques required for successful implementation.

Stephanie Quinton sat with her head in her hands at her desk. It was 10.30 am and she had already received three irate telephone calls that morning. One had been from her assistant food and beverage manager saying that he was two staff short in the coffee shop for the third day running; as a result he could not carry on much longer as all the other staff were beginning to complain about the extra work that they were having to do. The other calls were from customers. One had telephoned to inform Stephanie that after eating in the Victoria Restaurant the previous evening she had been ill with food poisoning and the other to complain about the poor service he had experienced when eating in the coffee shop the day before.

Stephanie had been food and beverage manager at Kirby Lodge, a small country hotel near Chard in Somerset, for only six months. In her time at the hotel, Stephanie had had to deal with an average of five complaints a day – from both staff and guests. She decided that the time had now come to take some action. At the next management meeting, on the coming Friday, she planned to raise the problem with Peter Randolph, the general manager.

Peter Randolph had been the general manager at the Lodge for two years. He was only thirty-six years old and it was his first general management position. He had been pleased to recruit Stephanie because she was well qualified, with an HND in Hotel and Catering Management and a good deal of industrial experience, having worked as a restaurant manager, as assistant food and beverage manager and a Manager for three leading hospitality companies before joining the Lodge. He was aware that there were problems in the food and beverage department but he was not aware of the full extent of these difficulties.

At the management meeting on Friday Stephanie brought up the problems she was having and suggested that perhaps she was not the only member of the management team experiencing such complaints from customers and staff. Philip Rhodes, the front office manager, was very sympathetic and was relieved to know that he was not the only manager dealing with such difficulties. Hans Schmidt, the head chef, said he had no problems and that he felt this was because of the way he managed the kitchen. The executive head housekeeper had been experiencing a number of similar problems to those mentioned by Stephanie. For example she said that only the previous day she had received two complaints from guests: one saying that the shower in her bathroom did not work, and the other that the extra blankets she had ordered had never arrived.

Peter Randolph listened carefully to the discussion. He recognised that Stephanie had raised an important issue and that immediate action was required. He asked his trainee manager, who had been present during the meeting, to carry out a small research project into the three departments currently experiencing difficulties, with the aim of ascertaining the six most common problems/complaints of customers and staff. It was decided that the report would be presented at the management meeting on the following Friday.

Greg Mason, the trainee manager, began his research by drawing up a list of all the staff who worked in the hotel. He then arranged to interview five people from each department over the following two weeks. Employees were to be selected according to age and length of service so that the sample would be representative of the workforce. At the end of the two weeks Greg analysed the data and produced the following pie charts to illustrate the main problems and complaints being made by staff and customers.

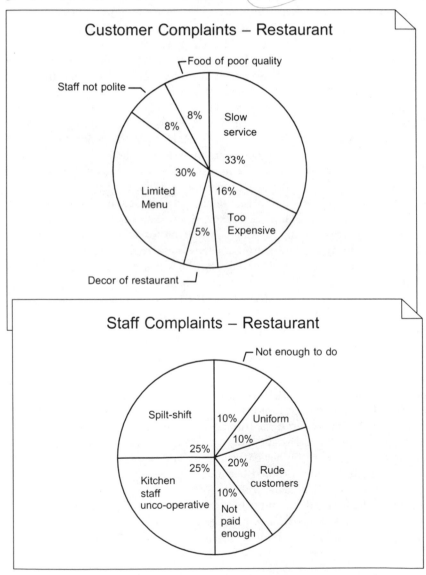

Customer Complaints – Housekeeping

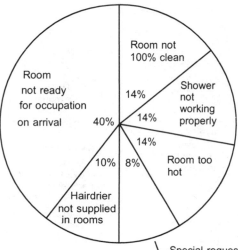

Staff Complaints – Housekeeping

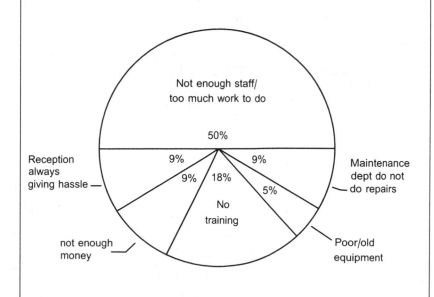

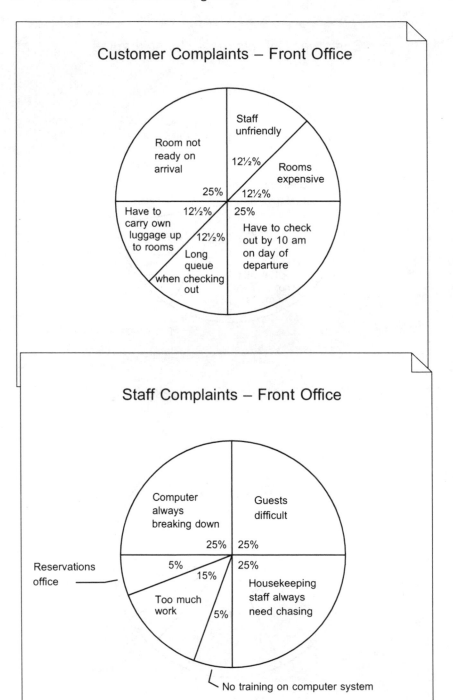

Customer Complaints – Front Office

Staff unfriendly
12½%

Room not ready on arrival

Rooms expensive

25%
12½%

Have to carry own luggage up to rooms
12½%

12½%
Long queue when checking out

25%

Have to check out by 10 am on day of departure

Staff Complaints – Front Office

Computer always breaking down

Guests difficult

25%   25%

Reservations office

5%
15%

25%

Too much work

5%

Housekeeping staff always need chasing

No training on computer system

Greg Mason presented his findings at the next management meeting. After some initial discussion the staff began to consider what steps they should take to combat the problems outlined by Greg's research.

The head chef suggested that Peter Randolph should call all the staff together from the departments experiencing problems and tell them that if staff performance did not improve immediately there would no longer be jobs for some people. The front office manager proposed a more positive solution. In his view, staff across all departments in the hotel should be invited to make suggestions about how the current operational problems could be solved, and particularly good ideas should be rewarded financially. Stephanie supported Peter's proposal and made the point that if the hotel was to solve its current problems it was vital that all staff were involved in the process. Greg agreed and proposed the setting up of quality circles, adding that he had read several articles in management journals as to how they had helped in the solution of similar problems. Peter Randolph said he liked the idea and would appoint an external consultant to advise on the setting up of a system of quality circles at Kirby Lodge.

As the external consultant, you have received the following brief from Peter Randolph. Please prepare a report based on the following points:

1. What are quality circles, and what factors must be taken into consideration when establishing them? *goals*
2. What are the benefits of using Quality Circles at Kirby Lodge? *How do you plan to achieve them?*
3. What are the problems that the hotel might encounter in establishing and operating quality circles?

Suppose Department heads

aims → plans

Points to be Considered when Dealing with this Case

Quality circles are just one vehicle for overcoming the problems highlighted in this case. When answering the questions you should consider the following:

(a)   The underlying philosophy of quality circles:

- Why were they first developed?
- What can they achieve that other management techniques cannot?

(b)   How do quality circles operate:

- Who is involved?
- What is their role?
- How often do they meet?
- What happens as a consequence?

(c)   The benefits with regard to customers, staff and the organisation.

(d)   The organisation of quality circles:

- Who sets them up?
- How are the staff selected?
- How do managers respond?

Part IV
Marketing

16   Travel Pal

Management Theme: Developing a Marketing Plan

Introduction

Hospitality companies operate in an increasingly competitive environment. As a result, marketing has become an essential part of any business activity. Organisations wishing to increase their sales need to carefully examine the market segments they are serving and the products and services they are offering.

Aims

To develop creative and business skills.

Competences Required for this Case

(a) Theoretical knowledge of product development strategies;

(b) Theoretical knowledge of marketing plan production; and

(c) Ability to interpret a practical situation and apply theoretical concepts effectively.

Best Value Hotels is a leading UK hotel chain with operations in Birming-ham, Luton, Derby, Watford and Manchester. The majority of Best Value's customers are business travellers who tend to use the hotels between Monday and Thursday. The hotels do attract some weekend business from the short-break market but not a great deal, primarily because most of the hotels are not in particularly attractive surroundings: most of the group's hotels are sited near motorways, airports or railway stations.

Rupert Hardwick, the sales manager for Best Value has noticed an overall decline in sales of 20 per cent over the past six months and realises that he must draw this to the attention of the senior management team if the company is to survive in the marketplace in the 1990s. He has been reading an article in the trade journal *Hospitality Future*, about the motorway catering market and in particular a company called Foodstop that has invested £30m over the past two years in a new motorway product. Rupert has thought for a long time that the company should review their product and the article convinced him that he was right. He decided to telephone Rebecca Knight, the marketing director of Best Value Hotels, and discuss his thoughts with her.

Rupert	Hello, Rebecca, it's Rupert from Sales. How are you?
Rebecca	Fine, thank you. Very busy, but how can I help you?
Rupert	It's about our sales. It's not that they aren't good, it's just that I don't think we are achieving the level of sales which we are capable of.
Rebecca	That's interesting. What have you in mind?
Rupert	Well, I've been monitoring our sales figures for six months now and I have noticed a continuing downward trend compared with last year's figures when the rate of inflation is taken into account. For instance, our room sales are down by 20 per cent and not surprisingly, so are our food and beverage sales. I have a few suggestions which I would like you to consider.
Rebecca	I always like people who have solutions to problems. In my experience such managers are rare. Please tell me your ideas.
Rupert	For some time now I've thought that we ought to expand our market. Instead of just concentrating on the business traveller we ought to be widening our appeal to include all types of traveller. We already have operations based near travel networks and all we

> need to do is review our product and develop a marketing strategy to attract new customers.
>
> **Rebecca** I like the sound of this, Rupert, but I think we need some more information before we go any further. I suggest we put your idea on the agenda for next week's sales and marketing meeting at head office, and the committee can put their views forward. In the meantime, I will ask Alex Joseph, our special projects officer, to draw up a report on the feasibility of Best Value moving into this market. Thank you for ringing me. I'll be in touch once I've spoken to Alex. He may want to come down and see you for a meeting.
>
> **Rupert** I am glad you like the idea and I'll be delighted to speak to Alex whenever he wants.
>
> **Rebecca** Leave it with me then, Rupert – I'll be in touch as soon as I've spoken to Alex.

Rebecca went to discuss the idea with Alex Joseph. Alex, although happy to help, said he could not do anything for Rebecca until the following month as he was busy with the advertising campaign for their new hotel which was being opened in Durham. He suggested that Rebecca should call you in, as you have been working as a graduate trainee manager with the company for the past twelve months and have shown a keen interest and ability in the marketing area. Rebecca agreed with this suggestion although she asked Alex to oversee the project.

The next day, after speaking to Rupert Hardwick, Alex Joseph sends you the following brief.

To: Management Trainee

From: Special Projects Officer, Head Office

I have spoken to Rebecca Knight and Rupert Hardwick about a new project they would like undertaken. Rupert has an idea about a new product we could offer called 'Travel Pal'. He has been looking at the sales figures for the last six months and is worried about the downward trend. 'Travel Pal' would be a complex offering budget accommodation for all types of traveller, plus catering facilities and possibly retail outlets etc. Before any discussions about this take place please can you do the following for me:

1.   Outline the factors we would need to take into consideration in developing such a new product.
2.   Develop an outline marketing plan for 'Travel Pal'.

Points to be Considered when Dealing with this Case

Marketing is an important part of a hospitality manager's job. In order to be successful a company must identify its market accurately and develop products and services to meet the needs of that market. In answering the questions to this case you should consider the following:

(a) The philosophy of marketing.

- What is it?
- What does it aim to achieve?
- How does it complement the other management disciplines?

(b) New product development.

- What steps are involved?
- Who is involved?
- How are new product ideas generated?

(c) Producing a marketing plan is an important task and yet it is neglected by many organisations.

- What does producing a marketing plan involve?
- What are the main sections?
- How should you approach the task?

17 Blaen Wern

Management Theme: Marketing Research, Advertising and Promotion

Introduction

Before new products are developed it is important that market research is undertaken in order to identify and meet the needs of the target market. Once a product has been developed it is essential that an effective advertising and sales promotion campaign is developed.

Aims

To develop market research and creative design skills, and creative ideas.

Competences Required for this Case

(a) Theoretical knowledge of market research methods and techniques;

(b) Theoretical knowledge of advertising and sales promotion strategies; and

(c) Ability to apply theory to practice.

Blaen Wern is a medium-sized hotel situated on the attractive Murdock estuary. The hotel took its name from the surrounding countryside, for 'blaen wern' means 'the place before the marsh'.

In 1987, the hotel was bought by Mr and Mrs Jones, to achieve their lifetime ambition of returning to Wales to run their own hotel. They had both worked in the hotel industry for over twenty years and had gained valuable experience in running similar hotels for one of the large hotel chains.

They had seen the hotel was for sale in *The Caterer* magazine and visited it before putting in an offer. In their view the hotel was not achieving its full potential because the current owners were reluctant to invest in additional rooms and a new restaurant. The hotel had been built at the turn of the century and was in need of a lot of decoration. This was reflected in the asking price of £395,000 which included all fixtures and fittings.

The Joneses financed the purchase by selling their £300,000 house in Worcester and borrowing the rest of the money. In 1987 interest rates were low and Wales was experiencing a tourist boom. Their bank manager was very sympathetic to the project and agreed to lend £150,000 as a term loan over twenty-five years. It was agreed that the loan would be at two per cent over the bank's base rate. In addition to this loan the Joneses also raised a £50,000 loan in Deutsch Marks through a finance broker. The loan was secured by a second mortgage over the property.

For the first two years Mr and Mrs Jones decided to make no structural changes to the hotel. Their first task was to set about ensuring that the hotel would have sufficient guests for the following summer. The hotel's marketing strategy was to try and encourage visitors from West Germany and the Scandinavian countries. Mrs Jones could speak German fluently and she had a working knowledge of Norwegian. During the winter months of 1987 she made frequent visits to travel agents and travel fairs in northern Europe with the aim of securing bookings for the following season. The hotel's location was excellent for people who liked climbing and mountaineering, with Cader Idris only a few miles distant and Snowdonia about an hour's drive away. In addition, the Murdock estuary was less than a mile from the hotel and a favourite location for local fishermen. There were beaches only five miles away. It was hoped that these facilities would appeal to people who liked active holidays.

While Mrs Jones made frequent trips to the Continent, Mr Jones began to reorganise the hotel. The previous owner had employed three permanent staff plus a pool of local part-time workers. This was not a satisfactory situation, as many of the staff were untrained and there was a high labour turnover rate. Mr and Mrs Jones knew from previous experience that

European tourists expected a high standard from hotels and so a number of additional permanent posts were created. This greatly increased the firm's wage costs but it did mean that the hotel could now consider applying for regrading in the future. All new staff were given job descriptions and encouraged to study for catering and management qualifications at the local college. By the spring of 1988, the hotel's organisation chart was as follows:

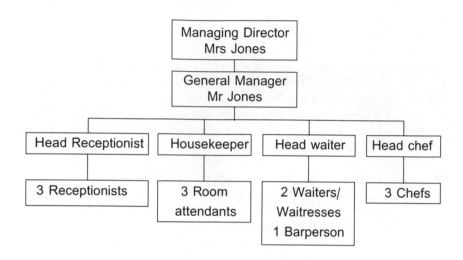

During the first quarter of 1988 trade had been slack. There had been a few travelling salespeople staying, but in the main the hotel had had to try and make its profit from its restaurant and bar. This meant that during the first quarter the hotel had experienced cash flow problems. These had, however, been anticipated and the hotel had been able to finance its day-to-day expenditure by operating an overdraft facility with the local bank on the understanding that it would be paid off once the new season's business began.

During the spring and summer months of 1988 the Blaen Wern hotel had nearly a 100 per cent occupancy rate. Many of the guests were from Britain, but Mrs Jones' hard work had resulted in the hotel having a large number of visitors from the EC countries too. By the end of the summer the hotel's receipts were ahead of its budgeted forecast and there was a small surplus at the bank.

But Mr and Mrs Jones knew that if their small cash balance was not to disappear they would have to attract more guests during the winter months. The problem was that most people in Britain preferred to stay at home between November and March, which meant that the hotel all but closed during the winter quarter. In an attempt to attract additional guests, the hotel marketed some short winter breaks at very keen prices. These proved to be fairly successful with the hotel achieving a 30 per cent occupancy rate during the winter quarter.

The restaurant and bar continued to make healthy profits and the number of corporate customers using the hotel for conferences and Christmas parties began to increase. Unfortunately, though, the hotel was not really suited to this type of business as it lacked both specialist facilities and the additional car parking space required.

The hotel was set in ten acres of attractive parkland. During the winter of 1989 Mr and Mrs Jones began to plan how they could turn part of the hotel into a conference centre with additional car-parking space. Their idea was to apply for planning permission to build a new conference centre with car parking space for another seventy cars. During the summer of 1989, a planning application was submitted to the local authority and, much to their delight, approval was given so long as the new building was built in the same style as the original hotel.

Mr and Mrs Jones have appointed a firm of management consultants to help them assess the viability of a new conference centre in this part of Wales. As a junior consultant with the firm you have been asked to prepare a report on the new conference centre proposals.

Memo

To: Management Trainee

From: Marketing Director, Capital

The owners of the Blaen Wern hotel are considering investing a large amount of money in a new conference centre. This centre will be able to accommodate 150 delegates and it will be set in some of the most attractive scenery in North Wales. The directors have appointed us to assist them with a market research study and to advise them on how the new conference centre should be promoted.

Next month I am meeting Mr and Mrs Jones and I would be pleased if you could prepare a report outlining the following:

1.   Prepare a draft questionnaire which can be circulated to past and present guests.
2.   Design a promotional brochure for the conference centre. The promotional budget is limited but will include four pages and three colour photographs. I am seeing a photographer next week but I need the basic design, layout and wording as soon as possible.
3 .   I need a short report outlining how the new conference centre should be promoted.

Thanks.

Points to be Considered when Dealing with this Case

Market research, advertising and sales promotion are all essential ingredients for an effective marketing campaign. In answering the questions you should consider the following:

(a)   What is market research?

- What are its objectives?
- What are the different methods?
- What are the advantages and disadvantages of each method?

(b)   What factors should be taken into consideration when drawing up a questionnaire?

(c)   What factors should be considered when designing a promotional brochure?

- Essential facts.
- 'Interest-raising' details.
- Presentation.
- Length.

(d)   What factors should be considered when producing a report on promotion?

- The reader.
- The decision-maker.
- Main sections.
- Length.

18 Crown Hotels

Management Theme: The Customer Concept and Customer Care

Introduction

Maintaining a high standard of service is an essential part of a hospitality manager's job, but as organisations grow and develop it becomes more difficult to control individual units. A particular problem faced by organisations incorporating franchisees is the issue of overseeing the operation and ensuring it meets the corporate standards.

Aims

To develop analytical and presentational skills.

Competences Required for this Case

(a) Understanding and applying the marketing concept;

(b) Ability to develop a programme; and

(c) Ability to apply theory to practice.

You have just been appointed marketing manager of the Crown Hotels group which has hotels in the UK, western Europe, North America and the Far East. The hotel group has become popular with corporate executives because of the range of business services the hotels can offer. Typing and word processing can be undertaken, faxes sent, documents photocopied and the hotel even offers a 24-hour courier service through an agreement with a famous worldwide courier firm.

The business segment of the market is beginning to account for an increasing proportion of the group's total sales and profits, but the main problem the Crown Hotel group has is ensuring that a business traveller staying at any of its owned or franchised hotels throughout the world receives identical treatment and standard of service. Internally, the company has always felt that the standard of customer care was higher at the hotels which it owned compared to the ones which were franchised. Unfortunately, a recent survey conducted by one of America's top business magazines has placed the company near the bottom of its ratings for consistency of service and customer care.

You arrived at work today to find this memo on your desk from the hotel's chief executive.

Memo

To: Marketing Manager

From: Chief Executive

Subject: US magazine survey results

I know that these people love finding fault but the hotel group can't tolerate results like these. We have always felt that there was a difference between the hotels which are owned by us and those that are operated on franchises, but that difference has never been so great as to put us near the bottom of the league before. Below are our group's ratings in the survey, which make dismal reading. The public relations department wants to reply but I have vetoed it. We don't need any more bad publicity. What I do need is some positive action so that when the magazine does its next annual survey we are reviewed in a more positive way.

I would like you to prepare a presentation for our next hotel managers' conference in Toronto outlining how our group can:

1.   Apply the marketing concept in all our hotels.

2.   Ensure that all our hotels are consistent in the standard of product and quality of service.

	Excellent	Good	Average	Poor	Unacceptable
Accommodation		*			
Food			*		
Staff				*	
Business facilities			*		
Customer care					*
Value for money				*	

Points to be Considered when Dealing with this Case

Customer care and good service are key issues in the hospitality industry. They are part of the 'marketing concept' which places great emphasis on the needs of the customer. One of the main difficulties is setting the correct standards and maintaining them once they have been established. When answering the questions to this case you should consider the following:

(a)   What is meant by the term 'marketing concept'?

- What are the key components?
- How does it affect the operation of a business?

(b)   How is good service established and maintained?

- How do you determine the required standards?
- How do you communicate these standards to staff?
- How can standards be measured?

19 The Cedar Tree Hotel

Management Theme: The Marketing Mix and Target Marketing

Introduction

Identifying new market opportunities is an ongoing management activity. Developing the optimum marketing mix and target marketing are important steps in the management of the marketing activity.

Aims

To develop creative and analytical skills.

Competences Required for this Case

(a) Theoretical knowledge of the marketing mix and target marketing;
(b) Ability to apply theoretical concepts to practical situations; and
(c) Understanding of the implications of the single market and UK hospitality organisations.

Robert Dyson picked up the Saturday newspaper and started to look at it before having breakfast. Managing a hotel was hard work and he liked to read the financial pages before starting work. As he turned the pages he suddenly saw an article in the holiday section featuring his family's hotel.

He had forgotten that the reporter had said it would be in the paper this week.

ADVENTURE HOLIDAYS
FOR THE SINGLE PARENT FAMILY

Where do you take your children if you're a young single parent wanting an adventure holiday for your children when you only have a limited budget? The answer is the Cedar Tree Hotel in Northumberland. Set in some of Britain's most attractive countryside the hotel specialises in providing reasonably priced holidays for single parent families. For prices at mid-season of £250 a week per adult and child you can have a complete rest while your child learns rock climbing, canoeing, camping and a whole range of other outdoor pursuits. Parents are welcome to join in too but most prefer to mix with other holidaymakers and just enjoy the beautiful countryside.

Robert and Jane Dyson started the hotel five years ago. Robert had just come out of the army as an instructor and had taken a job as an administrator for an electronics company. He didn't like his new job as he found it hard to work in an office all day and he missed being outdoors. His wife Jane continued to work as a voluntary social worker where she found that an increasing amount of her time was spent in helping and counselling single parent families. Jane realised that there was a need for a hotel specialising in holidays for this group of people. Many of the single parents were also lonely and wanted to meet other people but found it hard to socialise because of their work and family commitments.

Jane and Robert decided to set up a hotel for this market segment. They purchased a large country house in Northumberland which was set in fifty acres of grounds. Many of the first holidaymakers were acquaintances of Jane's but as time went by personal recommendation proved to be the best way of attracting new guests.

The hotel is planning to build an extension this year. People who would like this type of holiday should write to Cedar Tree Holidays, P.O. Box 342, Northumberland and ask for their free brochure.

Robert showed Jane the article. Jane commented that it was a pity there hadn't been more about their plans for a new swimming pool and mini golf course as well as the extension.

Robert smiled and told Jane that it would certainly help when he went to Hamburg the following month to market their hotel with the European Adventure Holiday Association. Their new brochure would be ready shortly and hopefully they would soon be getting a report from the consultant advising them on how to market the hotel in Europe.

Robert later phoned the consultant, Andrew Gardener. Unfortunately, he was not in his office, so Robert left the following message on his answerphone: 'Hello, Andrew, it's Robert from Cedar Tree Hotel. I haven't received your report yet and I do need to know:

1.   What the marketing mix is and how I should market the hotel in Europe?
2.   What is meant by target marketing and how we should position the hotel in the German market?'

As Andrew Gardener's personal assistant he has asked you to write a letter to Robert Dyson answering the above questions.

Points to be Considered when Dealing with this Case

Recognising new market opportunities is an important part of operating a business. Having found a new market it is vital that the right marketing mix is produced and that the market is accurately targeted. In answering the questions you should consider the following:

(a)   The marketing mix:

- Its components.
- How it can be varied.
- Factors to take into consideration when developing it.

(b)   Target marketing:

- What does it mean?
- What is its objectives?
- How can it be applied?

20　Truffles

Introduction

Franchising has become a popular method of operating business organisations in the hospitality industry. There are advantages for both the franchisor and the franchisee as well as the customer. In essence franchising allows the franchisor to develop the organisation at a rapid rate and gives the franchisee a well-developed product/service and support in operating the business.

Aims

To develop understanding of how to expand a business.

Competences Required for this Case

(a)　Theoretical knowledge of franchising and the single market; and

(b)　Ability to apply the theoretical concepts to a practical problem.

Truffles is a UK patisserie and confectionery restaurant chain which currently has seven units located in the south-east of the country. The chain was started by Louis Junot when he left the Clarence Hotel in London. He had been their chef patissier for ten years. Louis had always wanted his own restaurant and in order to raise enough capital he went into partnership with his cousin Henri. Henri had worked for a number of five-star hotels in Europe as a Restaurant Manager before coming to Britain to set up Truffles.

Henri and Louis developed a new restaurant concept by offering speciality pastries and chocolates as well as a full range of teas and coffees. The chocolates and pastries are all handmade and have proved very popular with customers.

Each restaurant has a seating capacity for approximately forty people. To date, Louis and Henri have been able to ensure that all their managers' have adopted the owners' management principles when running the restaurants and this is the main reason why the firm has not expanded as fast as it could have. Their aim has been to allow individual managers the freedom to manage while at the same time keeping a corporate identity for the restaurant chain.

Last month, their accountant, Ruth Weston, told Henri and Louis that the business was generating so much cash that they ought to consider investing in additional restaurants. She suggested that they become a franchise operation and open restaurants in the north of England and the European Community.

Henri and Louis know that many people are interested in managing their restaurants. Each week they receive at least ten letters from people living in Britain and other EC countries asking to operate a restaurant under a franchise agreement. They have decided to ask Ruth's advice, and wrote the letter shown on page 108.

Truffles
Cairns Street
Winchester
Hampshire
HS3 6GL

Dear Ms Weston

We were both very interested in your suggestion but we need to know more about the advantages and disadvantages of becoming a franchisor.

Also, we would like to move into the European market. What factors should we consider before deciding to locate Truffles restaurants in Europe?

We look forward to hearing from you soon.

Yours sincerely

Louis & Henri Junot

Louis and Henri Junot

Assuming the role of Ruth Weston, write a letter to Louis and Henri answering their questions.

Points to be Considered when Dealing with this Case

With the coming of the single market there will be even greater opportunities for UK businesses to compete in Europe. Franchising is just one way of expanding the business. In answering the question you should consider the following:

(a)   How a franchise agreement operates:

- The obligations and rights of the franchisor.
- The obligations and rights of the franchisee.
- The advantages/disadvantages of expanding the business by setting up a franchise agreement.

(b)   The single market

- The impact of the single market on business.
- The threats and opportunities posed by the single market.

Part V
Financial Management

21   The Riverside Inn

Management Theme: Raising Additional Finance

Introduction

The refurbishment of hotel and catering establishments is a necessary form of investment which has to be planned for. As new trends and fashions emerge with regard to interior design so managers need to ensure their units are up-to-date and inviting to customers. To do this requires effective financial planning.

Aims

To develop financial skills.

Competences Required for this Case

(a) Theoretical knowledge of the principles of cash flow forecasts, source and application of fund statements, and return on investments;
(b) Ability to apply theory to practice; and
(c) Ability to present financial information clearly and in the required format.

Lynn Stageman is the manager of the Riverside Inn. She is considering refurbishing her property and has written to her bank requesting a loan. She has just received the following letter:

National Bank
The Broadway
Worcester
WB1 7RT

Lynn Stageman
The Riverside Inn
Worcester
WH2 5KL

Dear Ms Stageman

Thank you very much for your letter requesting a bank loan of £90,000 over a fifteen year period to finance the refurbishment of the Riverside Inn.

I am pleased to be able to tell you that in principle the bank is happy to support your new investment, but I do need more information before I can grant the loan.

I would be pleased if you could supply me with an explanation regarding the company's source and use of funds, together with a statement showing the expected return from the investment and the profit-to-volume ratio of the proposed new venture.

I look forward to receiving this information from you shortly.

Yours sincerely

Barbara Holmes

Barbara Holmes
Corporate Lending Manager

Lynn then took the following action:

The Riverside Inn
Worcester
WH2 5KL

Hugh Smith
Institutional Management Consultants Ltd
Riverside Walk
Gloucester
GL3 4HF

Dear Hugh

I have approached the bank manager for the £90,000 loan and enclose her letter.

I would be pleased if you could prepare a report which I can take with me when I go to see Barbara next month which outlines why the money is needed and how the loan will be repaid. I am enclosing the latest source and application of funds statement. Barbara has told me that she will also want to see a report showing that the proposed investment is viable and the profit-to-volume ratio of the proposed new venture.

I look forward to receiving this information from you shortly.

Yours sincerely

Lynn Stageman

Lynn Stageman

Enc

Riverside Inn: Source and Application of Funds Statement for the Year Ending 5 May 1991

Source of Funds

Internally Generated Funds   £

	£	
Profit after tax		37,219
Add amounts not involving payments of funds		
Depreciation	24,348	
Deferred taxation	16,555	40,903
		78,122
Less dividend		12,631
Cash flow generated from trading		65,491

Application of Funds

Long-term applications

Net expenditure on fixed assets	41,795
Increase in funds	23,696

Short term sources and applications

	Sources	*Applications*
Increase in stocks		29,446
Increase in debtors		18,765
Increase in bank and cash		3,186
Increase in creditors	22,025	
Increase in bank overdraft	5,676	
Increase in working capital	23,696	
	51,397	51,397

Proposed Riverside Refurbishment Investment Plan

The aim is to completely redecorate the restaurant and to purchase new fixtures and fittings. I have had estimates for the work, which will cost £90,000, and enclose the forecast sales figures.

	Sales Forecast £	Variable Cost £
Year 1	45,000	21,250
Year 2	67,000	26,750
Year 3	84,000	41,000
Year 4	92,000	43,000
Year 5	99,000	47,500

The bank has agreed to a fixed-rate, interest-only loan of 14 per cent on capital borrowed for the first five years. Last year the firm's return on capital employed was 19 per cent and with interest rates at their current high rate I need to earn a return of 20 per cent from this new investment. I believe that the investment will have a life of five years and that it will have no residual value at the end of that time.

I have estimated that the fixed costs, excluding the interest repayments, will be £22,000 during the first year and that these will increase by 5 per cent per annum for the next four years.

Points to be Considered when Dealing with this Case

Financial control is an essential part of a hospitality manager's job. Effective control of working capital is dependent on accurate cash flow forecasting. The interpretation of a Source and Application of Funds Statement and being able to calculate return on investment and break-even points are important skills necessary for the successful operation of a business. In answering this question you should consider the following:

(a) Information revealed by the Source and Application of Funds Statement:

- Where the money has come from.
- How the money has been used.
- The company's present financial position.

(b) How to calculate the break-even point:

- What are the expected level of sales?
- What are the fixed costs?
- What are the variable costs?

(c) How to calculate the return on investment.

- What are the different methods?
- What are the advantages and disadvantages of each method?

22 Falmer School

Introduction

Apart from providing a consistently interesting menu, hospitality managers have to try to keep sales at a constant level.

Aims

To develop analytical, decision-making and costing skills.

Competences Required for this Case

(a) Theoretical knowledge of marginal costing techniques and break-even analysis; and
(b) Ability to apply theoretical concepts to practical situations.

118

Last year Falmer School for Girls decided to contract-out its catering as part of a cost reduction exercise. The traditional school meals had been unpopular with pupils for many years and market research studies showed that most pupils were in favour of some form of fast food restaurant.

At present the school has six hundred pupils of whom about 400 hundred choose to eat school meals in preference to bringing their own food.

Swan Caterers were awarded a three-year contract to manage the restaurant. During the first six months the restaurant offered hamburgers, pizzas and chicken nuggets. All meals were served with chips and no meal cost more than £1.50.

At first the restaurant was extremely popular with the pupils but as time went by many became tired of the lack of choice and sales have been falling. In an attempt to reverse this trend Swan Caterers have decided to expand the choice of meals by offering a range of three new salads. If this proves to be successful, soups and a new range of puddings will be introduced in the near future.

Swan Caterers' fixed costs of operating the restaurant are £60,000 a quarter. These costs includes staff costs and all the overheads involved in operating the restaurant. One problem for the firm is that during the school holidays there are no customers and so a high level of sales is needed during term time to compensate for this. The firm has calculated that its traditional fast food products will always cover 60 per cent of its fixed overheads but Swan Caterers are hoping that the new range of products will allow them to break even and become profitable. The selling prices and costs of the proposed new meals are shown below.

Salads	Beef	Chicken	Turkey
	£	£	£
Dish	0.78	0.65	0.57
Salad	0.45	0.35	0.40
Packaging	0.17	0.18	0.17
Direct Labour	0.25	0.25	0.20
Selling Price	2.99	2.65	2.59

The firm believes that each week during the Summer Term they can sell 200 salads and that they will sell in the following ratio:

Beef 5, Chicken 3, Turkey 2. Use this information to answer the following questions:

1. Calculate the contribution from each salad sold.

2. How many beef, chicken and turkey salads will need to be sold for the firm to cover its fixed costs?

3. What are the limitations of using break-even analysis?

Points to be Considered when Dealing with this Case

Day-to-day financial control is an essential management activity. Making decisions about the most profitable products to sell requires a thorough understanding of the concept of marginal costing. In answering this question you should consider the following:

(a) The importance of the term 'contribution':

- What it means.
- How it is calculated.
- How it can be used to make decisions.

(b) The break-even point.

- What it means.
- How it is calculated.
- How it can assist management in making pricing decisions.

23 Griffin Hotel and Leisure Group

Management Theme: Financial Control

Introduction

Interpreting financial information is a complex task for which hospitality managers need a sound financial base. It is therefore important that managers understand and are capable of applying financial control techniques when operating their businesses.

Aims

To develop skills in interpreting information and providing financial guidance.

Competences Required for this Case

(a) Theoretical knowledge of working capital management, source and application of fund statements, gearing and financial control systems;
(b) Ability to interpret financial information; and
(c) Ability to present a report clearly to non-financial managers.

Christopher Woodley sat back in his comfortable easy chair and turned on the television using the remote control switch. Christmas was over for another year. The children had enjoyed it and his wife Emma was delighted with her present of a new small car. Being the finance director of the Griffin Hotel and Leisure Group certainly had its benefits, even if it did mean frequent nights away from home and long hours at the office. Christopher reached out for the bottle of malt scotch on the table. Slowly he poured himself another drink and began to reflect on the past and coming years.

He had joined GHLG as their finance director in 1987 after being head-hunted by a firm of recruitment consultants. It was his first appointment at board level in a major Public Limited Company and the move had been very good, from both a career and financial point of view. The company had been in existence for over seventy years and had grown into a large hotel and leisure group: it owned hotels and restaurants, public houses, plus a marina and time-share apartments in Spain. Last year the group had a turnover of £520m and saw profits reach a record £57m.

Christopher had helped the firm to secure loans from a number of European banks to finance the marina in Spain, and had spent the rest of the year in talks with the group's merchant bankers about a possible rights or debenture issue.

Ever since he had joined the company he had felt that the firm should dispose of its three oldest hotels, located in Bristol, Bath and Gloucester. All these hotels were in need of refurbishment and were losing money. The new hotels which the group had acquired in key business locations were all performing well and Christopher had proposed to the board that the three old hotels should be sold.

At the start of 1990 the group began a major audit of its activities. The Chairwoman Helen Saunders, wanted to turn the company into a major European leisure group. The plan was to acquire new hotels in Europe, develop further time-share properties and dispose of all the unprofitable parts of the group. Christopher had agreed with her analysis and was pleased that she had relied on his financial expertise before embarking upon such an ambitious project. The sale of this division was accepted by the board in the spring of 1990.

When it was announced that the group was going to sell off its old hotels, financial analysts praised the company for its bold and dramatic reorganisation. The institutional investors had also been pleased, and the company's shares stood at an all time high of £5.25. Naturally enough, the managers and staff at the three old hotels were distressed at the news. This after all had been where the firm had begun, and in their minds it was lack of investment which had led to the poor financial returns of these three hotels.

The Bristol hotel was managed by Hugh Arnold. He had worked for the firm for over twenty-five years. On hearing the news he had contacted a firm specialising in financing management buy-outs. Hugh was determined to save his hotel and the other two also if possible, and had already approached Helen Saunders to find out if she would be prepared to consider a management buy-out for the three hotels. She agreed to put the matter to the board of directors' meeting in July.

Christopher Woodley had not been able to attend that meeting as he was in Germany. When he returned to Britain he heard that the board had decided to sell the three hotels for £2.56 m. As part of the deal the Griffin Hotel and Leisure Group would lend the new managers £1m for five years at a preferential interest rate of 12 per cent. The balance of the money would be financed by borrowing and from the savings of the new directors and workers.

Hugh Arnold planned to start a new small hotel chain and he approached Christopher to ask him if he would be interested in becoming the new managing director. Initially, the salary would be lower but he would receive shares in the new venture and would for the first time in his life be able to become his own boss. But if he accepted the post he would have to remortgage the family home and take up additional borrowings from the bank. His wife was worried about borrowing so much money and she loved their detached house set in a tranquil Berkshire village. However, it had risen dramatically in value, which meant that they had sufficient equity in the house to allow Christopher to proceed with the new business venture if that was what he really wanted.

Emma and Christopher spent many evenings discussing the benefits and drawbacks of the new post. Emma worked in the City for a major insurance company specialising in risk management. If the worst happened the family could live on her salary, but it might mean having to sell the house. In November they decided that Christopher should accept the job of managing director. He resigned from Griffin Hotel and Leisure Group in December to take up his new position from January.

Christopher had always had a good working relationship with the managing director of GHLG, who now offered to pay half the cost of a firm of management consultants to advise the new board members on how to market the new hotel group and to advise on a new name for the chain.

On his first day at work in the role of managing director, Christopher read the report from the consultants. Hugh had admitted to him that the hotels were in a bit of a mess, but felt a new managment team could put the firm on the road to recovery, and the consultant's report was similarly optimistic.

Some extracts from the report follow.

Griffin Group – Consultant's Report

Conclusion and Appendix

It is our considered opinion that the three hotels are financially viable. The Bath and Gloucester hotels are both currently losing money and should be refurbished as soon as possible. The hotel on the outskirts of Bath would, in our opinion, greatly benefit from the building of a small golf course and tennis courts. The Gloucester hotel should also be equipped with a new gymnasium and fitness centre.

The Bristol hotel is the only hotel which is currently profitable. The profits from this hotel should be used to finance the new investment.

The company is currently short of working capital. Our advice is to seek extra capital by mortgaging the freehold interest of either the Bath or the Bristol hotel. This should allow you to raise an additional £500,000 which would allow you to finance the new improvements and provide the additional working capital which the hotel group desperately needs. Unfortunately, this would make the company very highly geared and will probably be seen as a risky investment with interest rates at their current levels, but in our view the company cannot afford the losses which it is currently making and must be returned to profitablity as soon as possible.

Extract from final accounts.

Budgeted income and expenditure for the next financial year

	Gloucester £	Bath £	Bristol £
Sales	140,000	110,000	180,000
Less variable cost of operating	80,000	90,000	75,000
Less fixed costs	90,000	70,000	85,000
Profit/loss	(30,000)	(50,000)	20,000

A copy of the firm's balance sheet is shown below. While the company is currently short of working capital, it is fortunate in being strong in assets. Our advice is to borrow against these to finance the new investment programme.

As agreed, Ms Amanda Wright, our financial consultant, will attend your next board of directors meeting to explain any further points.

Consolidated balance sheet as at 1 May 1990

	1991 £	1990 £
Fixed assets		
Hotel buildings	1,750,000	1,750,000
Fixtures & fittings	700,000	700,000
Motor vehicles	50,000	30,000
Current assets		
Stock	300,000	240,000
Debtors	125,000	80,000
Cash	3,500	2,500
Current liabilities		
Creditors	85,000	50,000
Bank overdraft	125,000	90,000
Financed by	2,718,500	2,662,500
P & L account	68,500	62,500
Share capital	650,000	2,500,000
Secured loans	2,000,000	100,000
	2,718,500	2,662,500

Griffin Hotel and Leisure Group

Memo

To: Amanda Wright

From: Christopher Woodley

Next week is our next Board of Directors meeting. At it we are going to discuss our new strategy and approve our capital investment programme for the coming year. I have drafted some questions and I would be pleased if you could write a report which can be circulated to Board members at the next meeting.

1.   I need a report on the hotel's present financial position. Can you please draw up a source and application of funds flow statement and outline how we can conserve working capital during the current financial year.

2.   The firm's gearing ratio is very high at the moment. Can you write a report for the Board outlining the risks of being so highly geared and what steps the directors could take to reduce the company's current dependence on borrowed money.

3.   The Board are keen to implement new financial control procedures. Draft a report outlining what financial controls the firm should introduce.

Points to be Considered when Dealing with this Case

Managing finance effectively is often the key to operating a successful business. Managers therefore need to have the skills of analysing and interpreting financial information. In answering this question you should consider the following:

(a) The importance of working capital:

- How is it calculated?
- How can it be controlled?

(b) Producing a source and application of funds statement:

- What information is required?
- How should it be presented?
- What information does it contain?

(c) The importance of gearing:

- What is meant by the term 'highly' and 'lowly' geared companies?
- How can the level of gearing be controlled?
- How does borrowing affect the company?

(d) The installation of financial control systems:

- Why are they necessary?
- What form can they take?
- How are they monitored?

NOTES

24 Beinn Bhalgairean and Kinglass Hotels

Management Theme: Purchasing a Hotel

Introduction

Purchasing a hotel entails a vast financial investment. When buying a business the opportunity usually exists to compare a few available properties. An essential part of the process is the analysis of the past accounts of each business and assessment of their financial performance to date.

Aims

To develop skills in assessing financial accounts and decision-making.

Competences Required for this Case

(a) Theoretical knowledge of final accounts;
(b) Ability to interpret and compare financial performance; and
(c) Ability to present a logical and well argued case for selecting one particular option.

M and H Auctioneers
12 Glen Clunie
Edinburgh

Dear Mr Whiskin

Thank you for your letter enquiring about hotels for sale in the Strathclyde region of Scotland. At present we have two hotels for sale. They are the Beinn Bhalgairean Hotel in Inverlocky on the A85 and the Kinglass Hotel in Cleigh, just a few miles from Oban on the A816. Both hotels are set in attractive countryside and we would definitely recommend early viewing.

Both properties will be sold at our auction in June and I am enclosing the latest set of accounts for both hotels.

If I can be of any assistance please do not hesitate to contact me.

Yours sincerely

Catherine MacIntyre

Catherine MacIntyre
Property Investment Manager

The Beinn Bhalgairean Hotel
Balance sheet as at 5 April 1991

	Cost	Depreciation	Net Book Value
	£000	£000	£000
Fixed assets			
Freehold property	100	–	100
Fixtures and fittings	50	10	40
Motor vehicles	20	5	15
	170	15	155
Investments at cost			20
			175
Current assets			
Stock		30	
Debtors		19	
Bank		15	
Cash		2	66
			241
Liabilities			
Creditors		15	
Mortgage 2015 14%		30	
Net assets			45
			196
Financed by:			
8% preference shares of £1 each issued and fully paid		50	
100,000 £1 ordinary shares issued and fully paid		100	
Retained profits		46	
Capital employed			196

Notes to the accounts
Beinn Bhalgairean Hotel's earnings after tax (including earnings from investments) have been:

Year	£000
1987	33
1988	42
1989	37
1990	45
1991	41

The fixed assets have been revalued as follows by an independent valuer: Property: £130,000; Fixtures and fittings: £47,000; Motor vehicles: £12,000; and Stock: £28,000.

The average return on capital for hotels in this sector is 12% and the yield on comparable preference shares is 7%

The Kinglass Hotel

Balance sheet as at 5 April 1991

	Cost £000	Depreciation £000	Net Book Value £000
Fixed assets			
Freehold property	150	–	150
Fixtures and fittings	75	25	50
Motor vehicles	30	10	20
	255	35	220
Current assets			
Stock		17	
Debtors		15	
Bank		10	
Cash		2	44
			264
Liabilities			
Creditors		10	
Bank term loan 2015 15%		25	35
Net assets			229
Financed by:			
150,000 ordinary £1 shares issued and fully paid			150
Retained profits			79
Capital employed			229

Notes to the accounts

The Kinglass Hotel's earnings over the last five years have been, after tax:

Year	£000
1987	44
1988	30
1989	39
1990	50
1991	47

The fixed assets have been revalued as follows by an independent valuer: Property: £175,000; Fixtures and fittings: £65,000; Motor vehicles: £17,000; and Debtors: £14,000.

The average return on capital for hotels in this sector is 12%.

You are Mr Whiskin's financial adviser. You have just received a copy of the accounts and a copy of the letter from M and H Auctioneers. Mr Whiskin would like you to:

1. Calculate the price which he should be prepared to bid for each hotel at the auction.
2. Advise which is the better hotel to purchase using the financial data provided.
3. Suggest factors that Mr Whiskin should consider before investing in either hotel.

Points to be Considered when Dealing with this Case

Decision-making is an on-going management activity. Some decisions are more significant and long-term than others, and purchasing a hotel is perhaps the most important decision a manager will make. It is important that the task is approached in a logical way and the accounts analysed objectively. In answering this case you should consider the following:

(a) The financial performance of each hotel:

- Profitability.
- Working capital position.
- Volume of sales.
- Return on capital employed.

(b) Factors to consider before making a decision:

- Return on capital.
- Pay-back period.
- Cost of borrowing finance.
- The hotel's short-term and long-term potential.

25 The Catering Hire Company

Management Theme: Investment Appraisal

Introduction

When introducing new products it is important to assess the expected returns and compare these with the needs of the business. There are a variety of different methods for appraising an investment which need to be fully understood by the hospitality manager.

Aim

To develop judgemental and assessment skills.

Competences Required for this Case

(a) Theoretical knowledge of investment appraisal methods;

(b) Ability to apply theoretical concepts to a practical situation; and

(c) Ability to present a clear and concise report for the non-financial manager.

The Catering Hire Company was set up five years ago by two former catering students who realised that there was a growing market for hiring out specialist catering equipment for functions. At first the company hired out cutlery, glasses, tables, chairs and marquees but today it hires out everything from food mixers to tablecloths.

Each year the company directors determine their capital expenditure budgets. This year the directors have budgeted to spend £120,000 but possible suggestions far exceed this amount.

The new projects have been code-named capital investment projects and have been abbreviated to CIP1, CIP2, CIP3 and CIP4. The costs and expected cash inflows are shown below.

Projects

	CIP1 £	CIP2 £	CIP3 £	CIP4 £
Investment	80,000	40,000	50,000	75,000
Cash inflows				
Year 1	30,000	12,000	17,000	25,000
Year 2	42,000	19,000	24,000	34,000
Year 3	60,000	32,000	30,000	45,000
Year 4	55,000	40,500	36,000	38,000
Year 5	43,000	37,000	40,000	29,000
Year 6	–	25,000	–	17,000
Estimated residual value as % of investment	9	7	8	6

Past experience has taught the directors that each project requires an additional 6 per cent investment in working capital. The company is currently earning a return on capital employed of 18 per cent and the directors need these new investments to earn a similar return.

You work as a freelance financial adviser and have been asked to advise the firm about its proposed investments. The directors have asked for a report about their proposed new investments. Your report should contain information showing the pay-back periods, the accounting rate of return and the net present value of the new investments, together with a recommendation as to which project or projects the firm should invest in.

Points to be Considered when Dealing with this Case

Investment appraisal is a process that needs to be approached carefully so that expensive errors are avoided. In considering which method of investment appraisal to apply, managers need to know the advantages and disadvantages of each method. In answering this question you should consider the following:

> (a) The different methods of investment appraisal:
>
> - The advantages and disadvantages of each method.
> - Factors which must be taken into consideration before a decision can be made.

Part VI
Operations Management

26 City of Lights Hotel

Management Theme: Project Planning

Introduction

Planning new projects is a task which involves the co-ordination and management of a number of variables. There are a variety of operational management techniques available to managers to assist them in the planning process.

Aims

To develop skills in using operations management techniques.

Competences Required for this Case

(a) Theoretical knowledge of node network and critical path analysis;
(b) Ability to apply these techniques to a practical situation; and
(c) Ability to produce a clear and lucid report.

City of Lights Hotel is situated about five miles from Heathrow Airport. The hotel is part of the City Hotel chain and they are considering investing £1.5m in a banqueting suite. The management of the hotel realise that this will force them to close part of the hotel for a short time during the building programme. The directors of the company have received tenders from two companies, Hotel Construction Limited and The General Building Company.

As part of the tender, both companies have been asked to provide a breakdown of the time needed to finish the job, together with the costs involved.

Last year you joined the City Hotels group as a management trainee and are currently working in the operational research department at the firm's head office. You have just received the following memo from your manager. The relevant correspondence is also shown. *See overleaf.*

To: Management Trainee

From: Operations Manager

Re: Building work at City of Lights Hotel.

I am attaching the quotes from the two companies. Both companies have stated the cost and time needed to complete the work but I would like the following information for the next directors' meeting which is scheduled for ten days' time. I need to have:

1.   A chart using node network showing the earliest and latest finishing times for both companies.

2.   The critical path for the project.

3.   A report to the directors stating which company we should choose.

Hotel Construction Ltd
Construction House
The Avenue
Malvern

Dear Sir

We are pleased to submit our tender for the banqueting suite at the City of Lights Hotel. Our tender includes a breakdown of the work which needs to be carried out, plus the cost of each stage. All our prices are inclusive of Value Added Tax.

Activity	Immediate Preceding Activity	Days	Cost £
A	–	9	12,000
B	–	21	45,500
C	–	15	32,000
D	A	6	8,000
E	A	21	47,000
F	D	24	56,000
G	E,F	12	17,000
H	B,C,E,F	15	14,000
I	C	21	49,500
J	G,H,I	15	73,000
K	J	21	22,000

We look forward to hearing from you soon.

Yours faithfully

B. Marshall

Brian Marshall
Head of Construction and Planning

The General Construction Company
212–216 Kingsdown Road
New Malden
Surrey

Dear Sir

I am enclosing our tender which includes a breakdown of the costs and time for the project. Our costs are exclusive of Value Added Tax.

Activity	Immediate Preceding Activity	Days	Cost £
A	–	6	10,000
B	–	14	48,000
C	–	10	27,000
D	A	4	7,500
E	A	14	49,500
F	D	16	55,000
G	E,F	8	19,000
H	B,C,E,F	10	13,500
I	C	14	54,000
J	G,H,I	16	69,000
K	J	24	17,000

We are confident that our years of experience in this type of work will mean that we can meet your deadlines and we look forward to receiving your instructions in the near future.

Yours faithfully

Pamela Goulden

Pamela Goulden
Marketing Director

Points to be Considered when Dealing with this Case

Hospitality managers need to have the skills to apply operational research techniques to project development. Managers are now working in an environment where new technology coupled with operational techniques can assist management planning and decision-making. In answering this question you should consider the following:

(a) What is the objective of node network?

- How does it function?
- What information is required?
- How does it assist managers?

(b) What is the objective of critical path analysis?

- How does it function?
- What information is required?
- How does it assist managers?

(c) What should be contained in the report?

- Who will be reading it?
- What key points need to be included?
- How should it be presented?

27 The Salad Bowl

Management Theme: Time Series

Introduction

Statistical analysis can be a very useful management tool. Time series can be applied to different situations in the hospitality industry and can therefore contribute to effective management.

Aims

To develop statistical and entrepreneurial skills.

Competences Required for this Case

(a) Theoretical knowledge of time-series analysis;
(b) Ability to apply theoretical concepts to a practical problem; and
(c) Ability to interpret and evaluate statistical information.

Gemma Braithwaite is the owner-manager of The Salad Bowl restaurant in London's Covent Garden. The restaurant offers both a 'take-away' and 'eat-in' service and all its products are cooked on the premises by Fran Lewis, a Cordon Bleu cook. The restaurant specialises in healthy dishes and it always has on its menu a wide variety of salads plus vegetarian quiches, casseroles and pasta dishes.

Gemma has never managed a business before and she is tending to 'learn by experience'. One of her problems is establishing the right staffing levels. She has noticed that there are definite peaks and troughs in the level of business achieved by the restaurant. As a result Gemma has not always been successful in having the right number of staff working in the kitchen or in the restaurant at the right time, thereby leading to overstaffing on some occasions and understaffing on others, and obviously neither of these situations is good. In the first case it means that the labour costs are too high, and in the second, customer service suffers. Gemma cannot afford either of these situations to occur too often as there is too much competition from two rival establishments, The Brunch Bar and The Snack House.

Gemma has been advised by a friend who owns a wine bar in the City of London that she should try and monitor the number of customers eating at The Salad Bowl over a three-week period. From this he believes it should be possible to predict customer flows. Gemma has decided to follow his advice and three weeks later she has the following information.

Day of Week	Attendance
Sunday	1052
Monday	731
Tuesday	794
Wednesday	842
Thursday	648
Friday	1165
Saturday	1375
Sunday	1038
Monday	761
Tuesday	800
Wednesday	875
Thursday	691
Friday	1107
Saturday	1429
Sunday	1009
Monday	768
Tuesday	779
Wednesday	887
Thursday	667
Friday	1170
Saturday	1454

Using the above data, calculate the firm's secular trend. Do you think that daily information is adequate for counter server level planning? If not, what extra information would you wish to collect and how would you use it?

Points to be Considered when Dealing with this Case

Hospitality managers have to produce results whilst at the same time controlling the use of human and financial resources. Time-series analysis can help in determining staffing levels. In answering this question you should consider the following:

(a) What is the objective of time-series analysis?

- How does it function?
- What information is required?
- How does it assist hospitality managers?

(b) What are the possible applications of time-series analysis to:

- Food and beverage departments.
- Front office and accommodation departments.

28 Fit-For-Living Leisure Centre

Management Theme: Linear Regression

Introduction

Assessing whether or not to invest in a new restaurant is a difficult task. In order to assist managers facing this task, linear regression can be used where the appropriate information is available.

Aims

To develop skills in applying the technique of linear regression.

Competences Required for this Case

(a) Theoretical knowledge of linear regression and its uses;
(b) Ability to apply it to a practical problem; and
(c) Ability to produce a clear and concise memo highlighting the main points.

Brian Kershaw is the catering service manager of the Fit-For-Living Leisure Centre in Rochdale. Currently the centre offers a confectionery and cold drinks vending service for customers. Brian has noticed that many of the customers ask at the ticket office where the restaurant is. Whilst Brian thinks there will be enough demand for a restaurant to be financially viable, he realises that he needs to have a reasonably sound forecast of expected sales revenue from a restaurant if he is to convince the head office that they should invest more capital in the restaurant.

Brian believes that a new fast-food operation should be added, offering such products as waffles, burgers, pizzas, milk shakes and fruit juices. He would like the new operation to be called 'Sizzles'.

The only data which is readily available relates to sales at the new restaurant facilities which the Fit-For-Living group have just opened at Harlow. The Harlow centre is used by about 2000 people a week and the cost of providing the service at Harlow amounts to 50 per cent of takings plus fixed costs of £1000 a week.

Weekly Usage of Centre	Restaurant Takings (£)
2000	3000
2200	2800
2400	3400
3000	4800
2600	4000
2000	2800
2400	3800
1600	2800
3200	5200

You are currently working at the Rochdale centre as part of your industrial work experience. Brian has asked you to:

1. Use linear regression to estimate the relationship between usage and takings, and to evaluate the restaurant proposal on the basis of the data given.

2. Write a memo explaining what other factors you would wish to consider in your analysis if data were available.

Points to be Considered when Dealing with this Case

Linear regression is a useful operational management technique to be able to use. Hospitality managers need to understand what it involves and how it can be used. In answering this question you should consider the following:

(a) What is the objective of linear regression?

- How does it function?
- What information is required?
- How does it assist hospitality managers?

(b) What are the possible applications of linear regression to:

- Food and beverage departments?
- Front office and accommodation departments?

29 The Seven Bridges

Management Theme: Using Averages

Introduction

When determining new pay rates it is often useful to know the average rate of pay in the industry. The manager, however, must realise that averages can be calculated in different ways and that this will have important implications when using averages as a basis for making decisions.

Aims

To develop skills in calculating averages

Competences Required for this Case

(a) Theoretical knowledge of the mode, median and mean;

(b) Ability to apply quantitative data to a practical problem; and

(c) Ability to produce a clear report.

Southwark Brewery is a small independent brewery which owns seven public houses close to the major bridges over the River Thames. Each year it has to review its weekly wage rates for bar staff. The new finance director has been looking at the firm's wage costs for the coming year and has calculated that last year staff average weekly wages were as follows:

Weekly Wage (£)	Number of Staff
180–189	6
190–199	7
200–209	10
210–219	8
220–229	7
230–239	6
240–249	4
250–259	3
260–269	2

The company know that the average wage in the industry is £190 a week. You are working at head office as a management trainee and have been asked by the finance director to calculate:

1. The staff modal, median and arithmetical mean earnings during the last financial year; and to
2. Write a report to the directors outlining which method would be most appropriate for calculating average earnings.

Points to be Considered when Dealing with this Case

Calculating averages is a frequent management task. It is important that managers know the advantages and disadvantages of using each method of calculating an average and that they can apply this to everyday situations. In answering this question you should consider the following:

(a) How is each method calculated?

- Mode.
- Median.
- Mean.

(b) What are the advantages and disadvantages of each method?

(c) How should the report be presented?

- Who will be reading it?
- How should the data be interpreted and analysed?

30 The Rice House

Management Theme: Estimating

Introduction

Estimating sales levels is an on-going management activity. As a result, hospitality managers need to be able to be as accurate as possible in their estimating.

Aims

To develop skills in applying estimating techniques effectively.

Competences Required for this Case

(a) Theoretical knowledge of 'absolute errors', 'mean' and 'standard' deviation;
(b) Ability to apply these concepts to practical situations; and
(c) Ability to interpret and comment on results.

The Rice House is a chain of restaurants specialising in oriental cuisine. Customers can choose Malaysian, Indian, Thai, Burmese and Chinese dishes. The food can be eaten either on the premises or taken away.

The first restaurant was set up in Manchester by Mr and Mrs Wong when they came to Britain from Hong Kong. During the last ten years they have seen their business grow from one small restaurant to a chain of eight restaurants in the north-west of England. Mr and Mrs Wong are considering opening two new restaurants in the Midlands with the aim of eventually becoming a nationwide chain.

Mr and Mrs Wong intend to finance the new restaurants by borrowing from the bank. The bank manager has asked them to estimate next year's sales, and past experience has shown that they are usually correct to the nearest £25,000. The budgeted figures are shown below:

Restaurant Location	Estimated Sales £
Manchester	425,000
Liverpool	195,000
Bolton	190,000
Southport	150,000
Leeds	175,000
Preston	250,000
Wolverhampton	125,000
Birmingham	100,000

Mr and Mrs Wong would like to know:

1. The maximum absolute error in the sales estimates.
2. The mean and standard deviation.
3. The spread of the data (and comment on its skewness).

Points to be Considered when Dealing with this Case

Estimating is an important process. It needs to be carried out carefully using techniques available to provide an accurate result. In answering this question you should consider the following:

(a) What is the meaning of:

- Absolute error?
- Mean and standard deviation?

(b) How they are calculated?

- What information is required?

(c) How can these techniques be applied to:

- Food and beverage departments?
- Front office and accommodation departments?

(d) What are the benefits to managers?